MW00977537

SAILING ACROSS THE CONTENT AREAS WITH LITERACY STRATEGIES IN THE ELEMENTARY GRADES

Alice F. Snyder

Debra J. Coffey

Kennesaw State University

Kendall Hunt
publishing company

Cover image © Shutterstock, Inc.

Kendall Hunt
publishing company

www.kendallhunt.com
Send all inquiries to:
4050 Westmark Drive
Dubuque, IA 52004-1840

Printed in the United States of America
10 9 8 7 6 5 4 3 2 1

About the Authors

Dr. Alice F. Snyder is an Associate Professor of Language and Literacy at Kennesaw State University where she teaches undergraduate and graduate courses in reading, language arts, and social studies methods. Her passion for children's literature is shown through her eight-year service as Coordinator of KSU's Annual Conference on Literature for Children and Young Adults in which she promoted the use of children's literature in K–12 classrooms. In addition, she developed and teaches a popular honors course, *Roots of Folktales: An Interdisciplinary Approach,* which explores folktales from around the world from historical, geographical, sociological, and cultural perspectives. Alice received awards for distinguished teaching, scholarship, and service from the Bagwell College of Education and Cambridge Who's Who. She is a co-advisor for the KSU Student Reading Council and Pi Lambda Theta. Alice's research interests include vocabulary and comprehension development, and implementing literature circles to foster motivation to read. She is currently engaged in a multiple state research project with several literacy experts to investigate the roles of elementary schoolpersonnel in the Response to Intervention process. Her research and service work has extended internationally to Nigeria, Ecuador, Mexico City, and Belize where she has taught courses and given professional development workshops to pre-service and in-service teachers. Alice has published *Reading Psychology* and the international publication *Education for Millennium Development.* She is the author of the strategy book *Research-Based Strategies for Literacy Instruction in Grades 3–5* and co-author of *Unlocking the Power of Language: Research-Based Strategies for Language Development.*

Dr. Debra J. Coffey is an Associate Professor of Language and Literacy at Kennesaw State University. She is an avid researcher who presents innovative pedagogy during national and international conferences, including the Oxford Round Table in England. During teaching experiences, she enjoyed seeing students from preschool to twelfth grade enter the world of a book and become enthralled with the learning process. Debra co-authored the book *Unlocking the Power of Language: Research Based Strategies for Language Development.* She is co-editor of the online journal *Taking Teaching and Learning Seriously,* she is a lead coach who serves on editorial boards, and she conducts international workshops for teachers. She received awards for distinguished scholarship and professional service from the Bagwell College of Education, Madison Who's Who, Cambridge Who's Who, and the Princeton Global Network. As a co-advisor for the KSU Student Reading Council, Pi Lambda Theta, and the Bagwell College of Education Graduate Student Association, she conducts literacy projects with pre-service and in-service teachers, and they have given 4,817 books to local outreach programs and partnership schools in Nigeria, Belize, Mexico, Costa Rica, and Ecuador. As Vice-President of Research for the Kennesaw Mountain Chapter of Phi Delta Kappa, her cutting-edge research focuses on literacy strategies to connect theory with practice. Dr. Coffey is the Director of the Center for Literacy and Learning in the Bagwell College of Education where she supervises mentoring programs to enhance the success of teachers and P–12 learners.

Dedication and Acknowledgements

This book is dedicated to the students of Kennesaw State University who have and will become excellent reading teachers. We wish them great success with every aspect of literacy instruction, and we know they will have a positive impact on children for years to come!

We would specifically like to thank three graduate students at Kennesaw State University for their support and encouragement throughout the writing of this book. A special thank you goes to former graduate students, Katie Biello, Allison Johnson, and Beth Midkiff, and their 4th and 5th graders in 2011 at Keheley Elementary School in Kennesaw, Georgia, who utilized Dr. Snyder's paraphrasing and note taking method, found it to be effective and easy to learn, and thus, gave it a new name—*SNAP! Simple Notes Are Perfect!* Thanks so much for your creative insights!

We emphasize the importance of reading and strategy guides in our literacy methods classes and have enjoyed collaborating with our students as they created these guides through the years. We would like to express our sincere appreciation to Dr. Snyder's former undergraduate students, Penny Kirkpatrick, Amy Pope, Christopher Brown, Brittni Chafin, and Steven Acquafresca for allowing us to include their excellent reading and strategy guides in this book.

We would like to thank our editors, Sarah Flynn and Katie Wendler, for their excellent support and feedback as we collaborated throughout the writing of this book.

A.F.S. & D.J.C.

Chapter One: Vocabulary Strategies to Enhance Content Literacy Instruction

The vocabulary strategies presented in Chapter One provide multiple opportunities for teachers to help students learn the meanings of words in all content areas through contextual, morphemic, and conceptual means. Research conducted by literacy experts such as Isabel Beck, William Nagy, and Edgar Dale have informed literacy practice in classrooms across the nation and the world with regards to vocabulary instruction. These key researchers have left an indelible mark on us and other teacher educators who strive to prepare teachers to meet the needs of English language learners and all children. These strategies serve as vehicles to help teachers develop expertise in moving students through their levels of word knowledge as they begin to delve more deeply into word meanings rather than simply exploring words on a surface level. Ultimately, these strategies impact student achievement by helping students to become independent learners and strategic wordsmiths.

Chapter Two: Instructional Strategies for Comprehension in the Content Areas

Chapter Two presents a variety of comprehension strategies that teachers may utilize to promote active engagement in constructing meaning in all content areas. They help students interact with informational text in a strategic manner which leads to more efficient learning from text. Literacy and cognitive researchers, such as Richard Anderson, P. David Pearson, Palinscar and Brown, Isabel Beck, and Margaret McKeown, have greatly influenced literacy instruction for effective comprehension for decades. These influential researchers have shaped literacy research and instruction for all learners. The strategies in this chapter are based on what research has taught us about levels of comprehension, cueing systems, the importance of activating background knowledge, and ensuring that students are engaged in an interactive way as they become critical readers who are able to strategically analyze text in order to learn more effectively. Thus, they not only know what they have read, but they realize the importance of the author's message and its potential significance in their lives. These strategies impact student achievement by helping students to become independent readers and consumers of print, and writers who think creatively and analytically.

Chapter Three: Strategic Reading and Study Guides in the Content Areas

The strategies presented in Chapter Three provide an array of innovative reading and study guides that teachers can use to promote strategic analysis of textbooks and other informational material in print, non-print, and online formats. The whole purpose of these reading guides/study guides is to facilitate the students' interaction with texts by guiding them through this process step-by-step or page-by-page. Literacy researchers and practitioners such as Karen Wood, Diane Lapp, and James Flood have made a positive impact on content area reading instruction for students of all ages by providing specific guides that identify and reinforce particular aspects of the reading process. Students who use these guides gain more confidence with the reading process as they capsulize and interpret what they read. Thus, they become more aware of what to emphasize or focus on as they explore the text. These guides provide a framework for effective study. As a result, students become strategic readers and learners who study more productively and experience higher levels of achievement.

Chapter Four: Strategies for Note Taking and Study Skills

Effective comprehension and strategic reading facilitates productive note taking and study in the content areas. Chapter Four provides a collection of practical strategies for developing note taking and study skills to promote strategic analysis of informational material. This analysis is essential for student achievement. Effective students not only read the material, but they are able to analyze it carefully and convey what they have learned. The note taking strategies in this chapter help students to identify and clearly convey what they learn from texts. These strategies, which are grounded in research, guide students through the developmental process of effective note taking. Study skills presented in this chapter facilitate students' ability to convey what they have learned and use it in various contexts, such as essays or multiple choice questions on tests. Additionally, study skills help students to process information for long term memory. This ensures student achievement and helps students to see the value of lifelong learning.

Chapter Five: Writing in the Content Areas

Chapter Five presents an overview of stages of writing development, writing assessment, approaches for teaching the writing process, and ways to conduct writing workshops across the content areas. Even though writing workshop emphasizes student choice in writing style and genre, today's expectations for teachers regarding writing instruction require creative approaches and planning on the part of K–8 teachers. The groundbreaking work of Donald Graves and Lucy Calkins has shaped writing instruction on many levels and has influenced us in our approach to teaching future and current teachers about writing instruction. On a more personal level, we were inspired by professors William G. Brozo, Janet Hickman, Lester Knight, and Jean Winsand, who emphasized process writing during our graduate studies. These educators emphasized the value of contextualized writing instruction in the content areas, and this chapter includes ideas for teaching the conventions of writing in meaningful contexts.

Writing and reading are intertwined, and they support each other for effective learning in the content areas. The ideas and activities in this chapter provide an assortment of instructional techniques for incorporating writing into instruction across the curriculum. This chapter presents ideas for using writing to assist with learning content-specific material, responding to content information, and writing to show learning. The creative instructional activities in Chapter Five are just a sample of the many research-based activities that inspire enthusiasm for student writing in the content areas. These activities help students to become lifelong learners who read and write for enjoyment and see the value of learning.

The Appendices provide additional resources that support content area reading and writing, such as a chart of the Common Core Standards for Language Arts, and an interdisciplinary activity that incorporates science, social studies, and language arts titled "Survival Island."

Alice F. Snyder & Debra J. Coffey

Contents

Vocabulary Strategies to Enhance Content Literacy Instruction   1

Instructional Strategies for Comprehension in the Content Areas   33

Strategic Reading and Study Guides in the Content Areas   65

Strategies for Note Taking and Study Skills   95

Writing in the Content Areas   113

Appendices

Vocabulary Strategies to Enhance Content Literacy Instruction

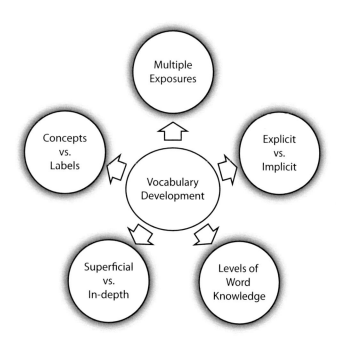

The vocabulary strategies presented in Chapter One provide multiple opportunities for teachers to help students learn the meanings of words in all content areas through contextual, morphemic, and conceptual means. Research conducted by literacy experts such as Isabel Beck, Margaret McKeown, and Linda Kucan (2002), William Nagy (1988), and Edgar Dale (1965) have informed literacy practice in classrooms across the nation and the world with regards to vocabulary instruction. These key researchers have left an indelible mark on us and other teacher educators who strive to prepare teachers to meet the needs of English language learners and all children. These strategies serve as vehicles to help teachers develop expertise in moving students through their levels of word knowledge as they begin to delve more deeply into word meanings rather than simply exploring words on a surface level. Ultimately, these strategies impact student achievement by helping students to become independent learners and strategic wordsmiths.

Word Knowledge Rating Scale

A great *before reading* informal assessment device, the word knowledge rating scale (WKRS) is used to determine a child's or group of children's prior knowledge of vocabulary that they will encounter in a text that will be read. Using Dale's Stages of Word Knowledge (1965), the teacher selects various words from the upcoming text, and places them down the left side of a table that is labeled with three of the stages of word knowledge (know it well, have seen or heard it, and unknown/no clue). The student checks the appropriate column for each word, depending on the level of word knowledge he/she has for each word listed. A fourth column is recommended, in which students write a short definition in their own words for the words they check as knowing very well, so the teacher can determine if the student does, indeed, have an understanding of the word as it is used in the text to be read. The WKRS is not graded.

Word Knowledge Rating Scale

Example below from: Ammon, R. (2000). *Conestoga wagons*. New York: Holiday House.

Word	Know it Well	Have seen or heard it	No clue!	If know it well, write a short definition in your own words
conestoga				
turnpike				
coaches				
terrain				
wagoner				
blacksmith				
wainwright				
cargo				
spokes				
wheelwright				
axle				
fellies				
circumference				
doused				
brakes				
mechanism				
teamster				
brake lever				
union				
tavern				
homespun				
draft horses				
massive				

Adapted from: Blachowicz, C. (1986). Making connections: Alternatives to the vocabulary notebook. *Journal of Reading, 29* (7), 643-649.

Word Knowledge Rating Scale for Grades 1–2

Directions: Use the happy faces to tell how well you know these words. This isn't a test and you won't be graded. Remember: You aren't supposed to know all the words.

I know it!

I think I've seen or heard it.

I don't know it.

_____ 1. waggling	_____ 8. debris
_____ 2. hermit crab	_____ 9. snails
_____ 3. sea anemone	_____ 10. sea urchin
_____ 4. lanternfish	_____ 11. prickly
_____ 5. starfish	_____ 12. murky
_____ 6. coral	_____ 13. barnacles
_____ 7. shell	_____ 14. flock

For the words you think you know, in the space below write what a meaning for each word is, in your own words.

Carle, E. (1987). *A house for hermit crab.* New York, NY: Scholastic, Inc.

Pictorial Semantic Web/Map

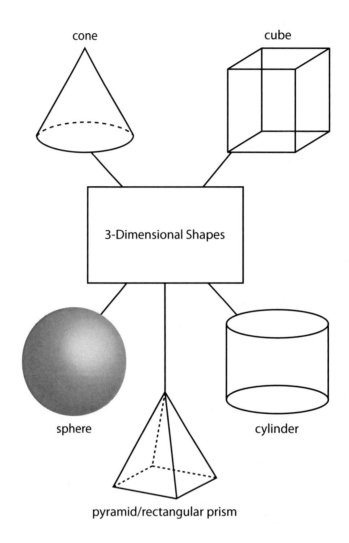

Semantic Word Map

Semantic word maps provide a graphic way for students to perform classification types of tasks for vocabulary learning as a step up from a pictorial concept map. In addition, semantic word webs/maps promote vocabulary development by helping students show relationships between concepts as they visually organize the information about the concepts.

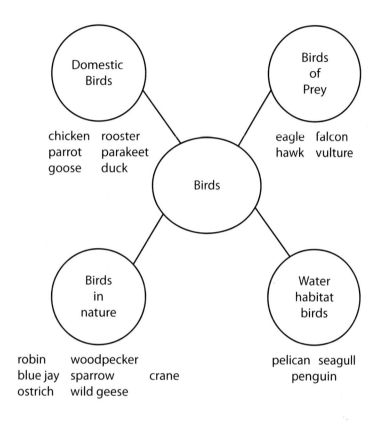

Example from: Snyder, A. F. (2009). *Research-based strategies for literacy instruction in grades 3–5*. Dubuque, IA: Kendall-Hunt Publishing.
*Semantic Webs by W. Nagy, adapted from Johnson and Pearson, 1984.

Classification

Learning vocabulary words that represent concepts should involve activities that require students to manipulate the labels for instructional concepts by thoroughly thinking about the technical terms of a given subject area. Four basic cognitive operations are involved: (1) *joining,* which takes place when students are asked to compare, classify, and generalize; (2) *excluding,* which occurs when students must distinguish among or discard items because they do not belong with the conceptual category being explored; (3) *selecting,* which takes place when students make choices and explain their decisions based on what they know, understand, or experience; and (4) *implying,* which occurs when students make decisions based on cause-effect relations among concepts or words. Implying as a cognitive function actually requires a combination of the first three operations due to the complexity of the task. Classification is a useful vocabulary strategy because it requires metacognition on the part of the learner as he/she engages in all four cognitive operations. See the examples below (created by Alice Snyder and Debra Coffey).

Directions: Read the list of words below. Think about how the words are similar and belong together. Write a word or phrase on the line that identifies what the words have in common.

triangle	crocodile
rectangle	snake
square	alligator
parallelogram	turtle
hexagon	lizard
octagon	gila monster
(polygons)	**(reptiles)**

Classification with the Intruder

Directions: Read the list of words below. All of the words in the list have something in common except one. On the line below, write the word or phrase that identifies what category or concept describes the words. Then shade the Intruder (word that doesn't belong).

punt	duck
pass	pigeon
tackle	robin
dribble	eagle
run	chicken
block	salamander
(American Football)	**(birds)**

Vacca, R. T., & Vacca, J. L. (1996). *Content area reading.* (5th ed.). New York, NY: Harper Collins.

Concept Circles

Concept Circles is an excellent instructional strategy for teaching vocabulary by relating words that exemplify a concept or category. Similar conceptually to categorization, students are required to determine how the words in the circle are related and then identify the concept or category depicted by the words in the circle. There are three different tasks that can be created with concept circles. The task directions must be included with each concept circle as well as a blank on which the child writes the concept.

The three tasks are:

1. What do all the words in the circle have in common? Write the concept or category on the line.
2. Shade in the section that contains a word that doesn't belong. Then identify what the other words have in common. Write the concept or category on the line.
3. What do all the words in the circle have in common? Write another word that goes with that concept/category. Write the concept/category on the line.

Hint: To create concept circles, it is easier first to think about the concept or category you want the students to identify. Then determine words that exemplify or are examples of that concept or category. Note that concept circles are not designed for activities in which students identify character traits or actions of characters/historical people and subsequently identify the character/ historical figure. Make sure children are able to determine the overall concept/category based on the words placed in the circle. The words must logically lead to the concept, as demonstrated in the examples on the next few pages.

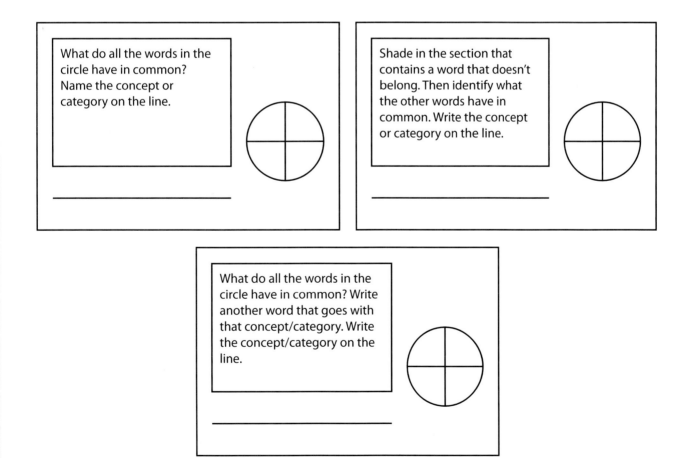

From: Vacca, R. T., & Vacca, J. L. (1996). *Content area reading.* (5th ed.). New York, NY: Harper Collins.

Concept Circles for Math and Science

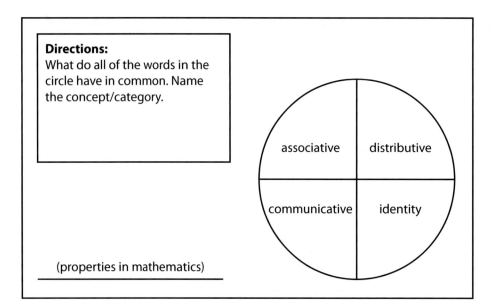

Directions:
What do all of the words in the circle have in common. Name the concept/category.

associative   distributive

communicative   identity

_____
(properties in mathematics)

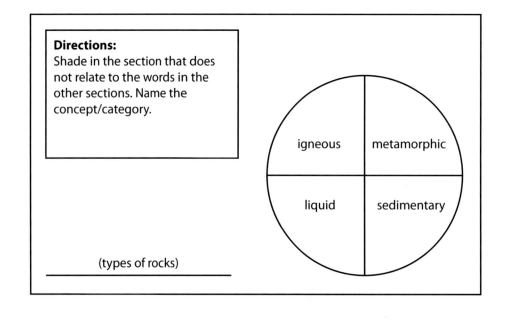

Directions:
Shade in the section that does not relate to the words in the other sections. Name the concept/category.

igneous   metamorphic

liquid   sedimentary

_____
(types of rocks)

Concept Circles for Social Studies and Health

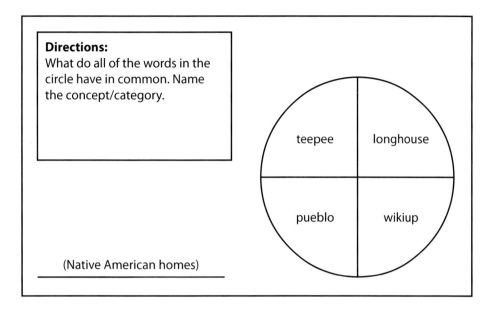

Directions:
What do all of the words in the circle have in common. Name the concept/category.

teepee | longhouse
pueblo | wikiup

_____ (Native American homes)

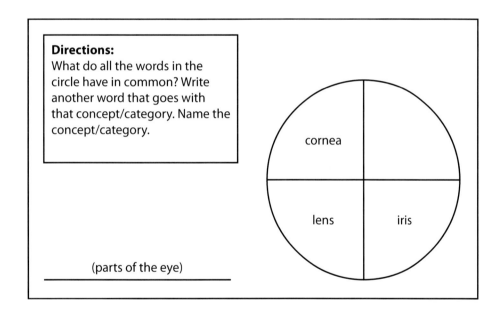

Directions:
What do all the words in the circle have in common? Write another word that goes with that concept/category. Name the concept/category.

cornea |
lens | iris

_____ (parts of the eye)

Concept of Definition Map

The Concept of Definition Map (CD Map) provides an organizational framework for learning conceptual information about vocabulary words that represent concepts. Three types of relationships are explored about a word using the CD Map. The first, categories, is explored by asking "What is it?" Students determine what category the term represents. The second relationship is properties, which is examined by asking "What is it like?" Students list three characteristics of the concept. The third relationship is illustrations, which is explored by asking "What are some examples?" Students list three concrete examples of the concept. Another feature of the CD Map is added by having students identify an example to compare the conceptual term or an example of an opposite of the term, in other words, "What is not an example of the concept?" or "What is the opposite of this concept?" See the blank example below:

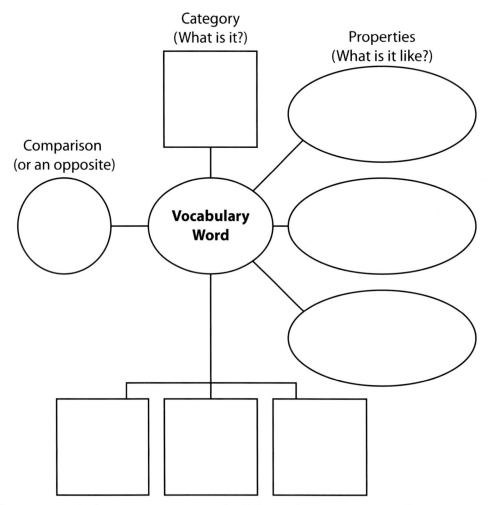

Illustrations: (What are some examples?) [actual concrete examples]

From Schwartz, R. M. (1988). Learning to learn vocabulary in content area textbooks. *Journal of Reading, 32,* 108–118.

Schwartz Concept of Definition Map

Science/Social Studies

sanctuary

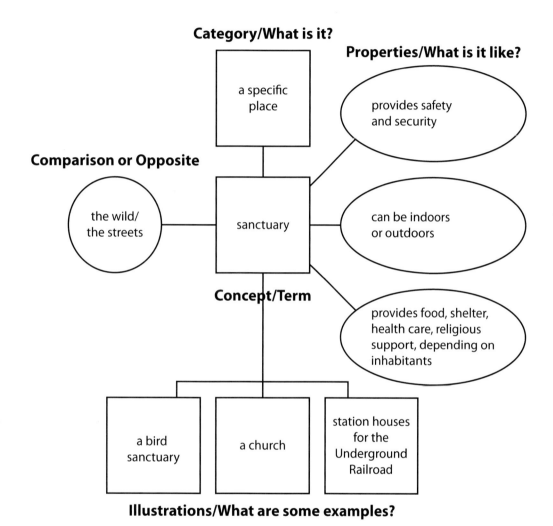

Category/What is it?

Properties/What is it like?

a specific place

provides safety and security

Comparison or Opposite

the wild/ the streets

sanctuary

can be indoors or outdoors

Concept/Term

provides food, shelter, health care, religious support, depending on inhabitants

a bird sanctuary

a church

station houses for the Underground Railroad

Illustrations/What are some examples?

Vocabulary word from: Hatkoff, I., Hatkoff, C., & Kahumbu, P. (2006). *Owen & Mzee.* New York, NY: Scholastic Press.

Concept of Definition Map (Schwartz)

Mathematics

cube

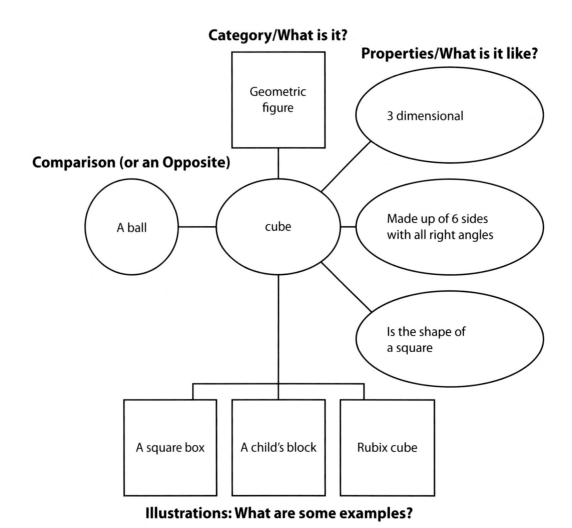

Concept of Definition Map (Schwartz)

Social Studies/Science

volcano

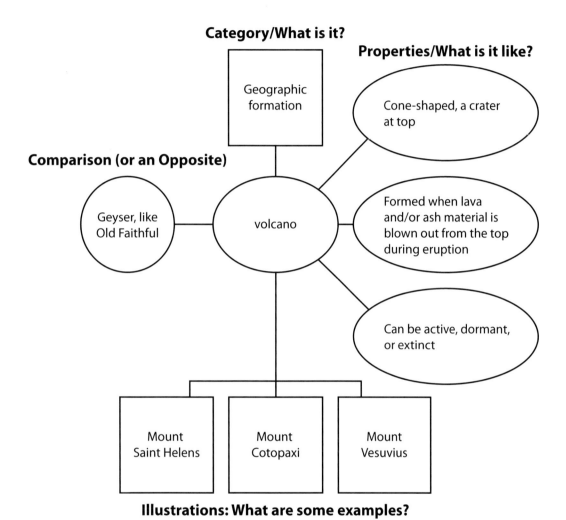

Word Bubbles

Word bubbles, developed by Bessie Haskins, provide a good review of conceptual content vocabulary. Word bubbles provide another opportunity for students to explore conceptual terms through multiple exposures in a variety of contexts (Beck, McKeown, & Omanson, 1987). Students are given one clue to the conceptual word's meaning on a line below the bubble. Using this clue and the list of words to be reviewed, they fill in the bubble with the concept term and list other clues on the lines for that concept. The example below was created for a third grade class.

Directions: Use the measurement word clue under each bubble to help you place the correct word from the word column in a bubble (in the example, "weight" will be the *concept* in the bubble). One clue word is given that helps you think of the concept "weight." Then add two more clue words on the blank lines extending below each line that describe the concept in the bubble.

Measure Your Words

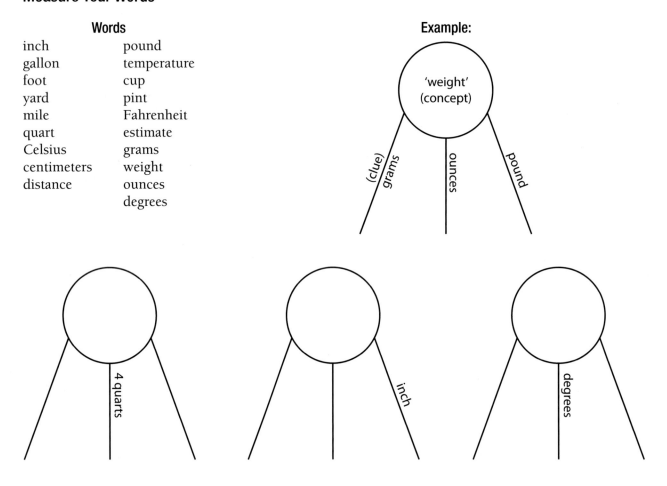

Words	
inch	pound
gallon	temperature
foot	cup
yard	pint
mile	Fahrenheit
quart	estimate
Celsius	grams
centimeters	weight
distance	ounces
	degrees

Example:

'weight' (concept)

(clue) grams   ounces   pound

4 quarts

inch

degrees

Developed by Bessie Haskins. Examples from: Richardson, J. S., Morgan, R. F., & Fleener, C. (2006). *Reading to learn in the content areas.* (6th ed.). Belmont, CA: Thomson Wadsworth.

Word Bubbles

Directions: Use the body system word clue under each bubble to help you place the correct word from the word column in the bubble (in the example, "nervous system" will be the concept placed in the bubble). One clue word is given that helps you think of the concept "nervous system." Then add two more clue words from the list on the blank lines extending below each bubble that describe the concept in the bubble.

Healthy Word Choices

Words

diaphragm	veins
brain	digestive system
lungs	spinal cord
neurons	bronchial tubes
stomach	respiratory system
arteries	heart
esophagus	circulatory system
intestines	nervous system

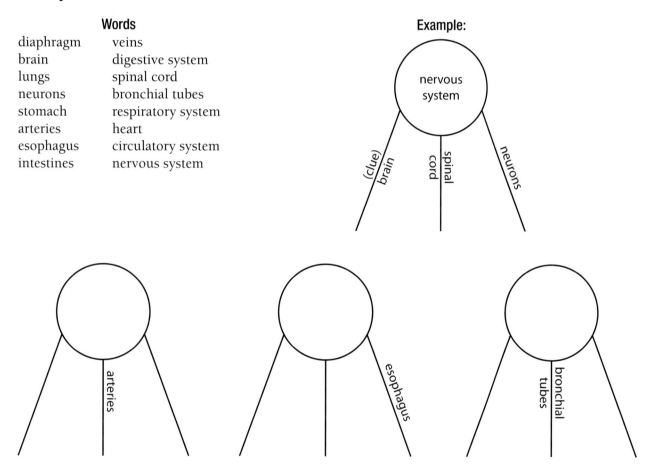

Developed by Bessie Haskins. Examples created by Alice F. Snyder and Debra J. Coffey.
Richardson, J. S., Morgan, R. F., & Fleener, C. (2006). *Reading to learn in the content areas.* (6th ed.). Belmont, CA: Thomson Wadsworth.

Word Splash

Example of a word splash with content vocabulary for *Owen and Mzee: The True Story of a Remarkable Friendship,* by Isabella Hatkoff, Craig Hatkoff, and Dr. Paula Kahumbu (2006, New York, Scholastic).

tortoise   **Mud Wallow**   companion

ecologist

coral reef

ANIMAL SANCTUARY

commotion

enclosure

caretaker   Swahili

POD

bushbacks   **hippopotamus**

protective presence

resilience

Word Splash:

A variety of words (5–15, depending on grade level) are written randomly across a paper (transparency) or chalkboard. If typed on a handout, it is useful to use a variety of text fonts and sizes. Most words are unknown vocabulary words, but a few might be more common words that will give clues about the content, characters, or setting (depending on what genre of book the words are taken from). A student chooses any word from the set and then gives a sentence or definition. The teacher expands with an example, steering the discussion to its usage in the text. Process continues until all words are discussed. Then the students are asked to predict the story or text information based on the words.

Adapted from Dorsey Hammond's Keyword Strategy

Frayer Model

Definition:	Sentence:
disagreement, dispute, or struggle resulting from a clash of ideas, interests, or emotions	The administrator was in conflict with his computer when he was facing a major deadline and the system froze.
Example:	**Non-Example:**
 Image © Minerva Studio, 2012. Used under license by Shutterstock, Inc.	 Image © Emil Durov, 2012. Used under license by Shutterstock, Inc.

Conflict

Frayer, D. A., Frederick, W. C., & Klausmeier, H. J. (1969). *A schema for testing the level of concept mastery.* Technical Report No. 16. Madison, WI: University of Wisconsin Research and Development Center for Cognitive Learning. Example created by Alice Snyder and Debra Coffey.

Vocabulary Illustrations/Vocabulary Pictures

Vocabulary Illustrations/Vocabulary Pictures provide students with opportunities to demonstrate word knowledge in creative ways. This strategy allows students to draw what they understand about word meanings. Students choose words or are given words for the activity. Then they write the words and their definitions on drawing paper. Students find pictures or draw pictures to illustrate the concepts or words. Below their pictures, students write sentences to clarify or go along with what is depicted in their pictures or drawings. Short definitions may be added for additional clarification.

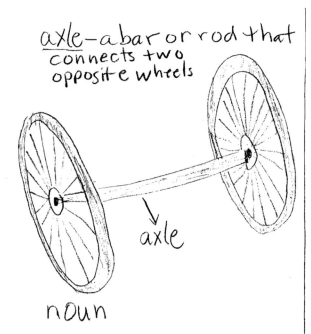

axle—a bar or rod that connects two opposite wheels

axle

noun

The axle on the front wheels of our wagon broke when we ran over the big hole in the trail.

terrain—a tract of land with its natural or topographic features

noun

The terrain was too rugged for the wagons to travel across so the pioneers had to take a different route that was flatter and easier to travel on.

Word Expert Cards

Word Expert Cards, created by Landsdown in 1991, allow children to combine drawing with various aspects of vocabulary learning from fiction and non-fiction texts. The teacher identifies a list of 50-100 key words from a chapter book or unit of study, using a combination of the content area textbook and various non-fiction and electronic texts. Each student receives 2-4 words from which to develop Word Expert Cards. The teacher writes a page number beside each word so students can find the words in the indicated text. Students are given sheets of construction paper to create a Word Expert Card for each word. **Directions** are given to students as follows:

1. Use the page number to locate the word in the story.
2. **Copy the sentence containing the word** inside the card.
3. Use a dictionary to look up the definition for each word; discuss it with others.
4. On scratch paper, write the **part of speech** and the **definition in your own words** that match the use of the word in the story.
5. Then, on the scratch paper, **write your own sentence using the word.**
6. Get the definition and sentence approved for accuracy by the teacher.
7. Copy onto the inside of your card the **approved** definition, part of speech, and sentence.
8. Write the vocabulary word on the front outside of the card in big bold letters.
9. On the front of the card, **illustrate the vocabulary word** neatly and creatively. Get your illustration approved before creating your final word expert cards.
10. Write your name and word on the back side of the card.

Examples (vocabulary words from *Conestoga Wagons*, by Richard Ammon, 2000):

Cargo—pg. 1
Sentence where found—Today the port of Philadelphia bustles as cranes unload **cargo** from ships onto waiting trucks and trains.
Part of Speech—noun
Definition—goods carried by a ship, aircraft, train, truck, or other vehicle; freight
My Own Sentence—For our trip west, we loaded our wagon with barrels full of **cargo** such as flour, pots and pans, and other household items we would need once we reached our destination.

Image © Elena Terletskaya, 2012. Used under license by Shutterstock, Inc.

Conestoga wagons—pgs. 1–2
Sentence where found—Between 1750 and 1850, goods were unloaded into **Conestoga wagons,** which served as the tractor-trailer trucks of that time.
Part of Speech—noun
Definition—a large, heavy, broad-wheeled covered wagon for transporting pioneers and freight across North America during early westward migration.
My Own Sentence—We loaded the cargo onto our **Conestoga wagon** to prepare for our journey across the vast prairie beyond the Mississippi.

Image © Dennis Cox, 2012. Used under license by Shutterstock, Inc.

Adapted from: Richek, M. A. (2005).Words are wonderful: Interactive, time-efficient strategies to teach meaning vocabulary, *The Reading Teacher, 58*(5), 414–423.

Vocabulary Venn Diagram

Revolution (Science/Social Studies)

Many words in our language have more than one meaning. A vocabulary Venn Diagram is a useful and simple way to show children these multiple meaning words. First, place the word that has at least two meanings in the intersected area of the Venn Diagram. Then ask children to determine other meanings of the word and place them in the circle areas that have not been intersected. Use a word or short phrases as references to the meanings.

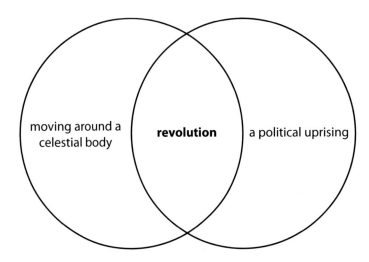

Vocabulary Venn Diagram

Muscle (Science)

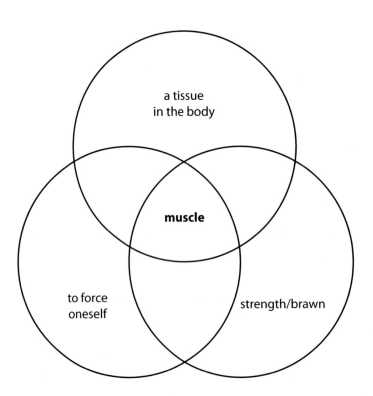

Magic Squares

Magic Squares is an instructional strategy that can be used at all levels, with content vocabulary and vocabulary found in children's literature. The Magic Square is a special arrangement of numbers that when added across, down, or diagonally always equals the same sum. Students match a series of definitions or word explanations (labeled with numbers) to the vocabulary placed in the squares. Students write the number of the definition that matches the word in the square. If their answers are correct, the sum of the numbers when added across, down, or diagonally will be the same.

Some possible magic square combinations:

8	1	6
3	5	7
4	9	2

15

6	7	2
1	5	9
8	3	4

15

9	2	7
4	6	8
5	10	3

18

5	4	9
10	6	2
3	8	7

18

16	2	3	13
5	11	10	8
9	7	6	12
4	14	15	1

34

4	9	5	16
14	7	11	2
15	6	10	3
1	12	8	13

34

Example of elementary grade magic square on the Ancient World: Developed by Ed Toscano.

Directions: Read each of the sentences below the magic square. Match the sentence to the correct word on the square. Put the number of the sentence in that box. If your answers are correct, the sum of the numbers when added across or down (or diagonally) will be the same.

Parthenon	Olympics	Slaves
———	———	———
Athens	Columns	Arches
———	———	———
Republic	Aqueduct	Rome
———	———	———

1. The sporting event the Greeks invented to help train warriors.
2. This city ruled the largest empire in the world.
3. This city was the largest direct democracy in the world.
4. The type of government where citizens elect people to represent them.
5. The Greeks invented these to build temples and other important buildings.
6. These people could win their freedom by fighting in the Coliseum.
7. The Romans invented these to provide strong support for buildings.
8. The name of the temple built to honor the goddess Athena.
9. This carried water from the mountains to the city.

Ancient World example from: Richardson, J. S., & Morgan, R. F. (2003). *Reading to learn in the content areas.* (5th ed.). Belmont, CA: Thomson Wadsworth Publishing.
Richardson, J. S., & Morgan, R. F. (2003). *Reading to learn in the content areas.* (5th ed.). Belmont, CA: Thomson Wadsworth Publishing.

Magic Squares

Landforms

Example of elementary grade Magic Square on different landforms around the world.

Directions: Read each of the sentences below the magic square. Match the sentence to the correct word on the square. Put the number of the sentence in that box. If your answers are correct, the sum of the numbers when added across or down (or diagonally) will be the same.

rainforest	tundra	desert
_____	_____	_____
mountain	coastal plain	plateau
_____	_____	_____
plain	wetlands	island
_____	_____	_____

1. This is a raised area on the earth's surface which may be rocky and rugged that is often created by turbulent forces on or within the earth, such as earthquakes, volcanoes, shifting tectonic plates, and erosion.
2. This is a region that is hot, dry, with little rainfall and abundant sand and dunes.
3. This is a lowland area, such as a marsh, that is saturated with moisture.
4. This is an area of land completely surrounded by water.
5. This is an area where low-lying land meets the ocean.
6. This is a dense evergreen forest in a tropical region that receives abundant rainfall.
7. This is an area of flat, treeless, frozen ground found in Arctic regions with low-growing vegetation.
8. This is an extensive, treeless area of relatively level land or rolling hills with tall grass.
9. This is an elevated, or raised, expanse of level land.

Example created by Alice Snyder and Debra Coffey. Adapted from: Richardson, J. S., & Morgan, R. F. (2003). *Reading to learn in the content areas*. (5th ed.). Belmont, CA: Thomson Wadsworth Publishing.

Semantic Feature Analysis (Word Matrix)

The Semantic Feature Analysis (Anders & Bos, 1986), or Word Matrix, is a useful graphic organizer for vocabulary development that helps students see the relationships among concepts and terms that may be found within a single text or between multiple texts. Grounded in schema theory (Rumelhart, 1980), this strategy can be used effectively before, during, and after reading about a particular topic. First, place the given vocabulary words down the left side of the matrix. Next, across the top, list specific features that the terms may or may not have in common. Then provide a code for how students should mark the boxes for each word when determining whether the word does or does not contain or demonstrate the feature.

The Solar System

	Is an Inner Planet	Is an Outer Planet	Has an Atmosphere	Supports life	Made of Rock and Metal	Made of Gas	Has Moons	Has Rings
Mercury	√	o	o	o	√	o	o	o
Venus	√	o	√	o	√	o	o	o
Earth	?	?	√	√	√	o	√	o
Mars	o	√	√	o	√	o	√	o
Jupiter	o	√	o	o	o	√	√	√
Saturn	o	√	o	o	√	o	√	√
Uranus	o	√	o	o	√	o	√	√
Neptune	o	√	o	o	√	o	√	o

Key: √ if yes   o if no   ? if not sure

Adapted from: Tompkins, G. E. (2003). *Literacy for the 21st century.* (3rd ed.). Upper Saddle River, NJ: Merrill Prentice-Hall.

Anders, P., & Bos, C. (1986). Semantic feature analysis: An interactive strategy for vocabulary development and text comprehension, *Journal of Reading, 29*(7), 610–616.

Rumelhart, D. E. (1980). Schemata: The building blocks of cognition. In R. J. Spiro, B. C. Bruce, & W. F. Brewer (Eds.), *Theoretical issues in reading comprehension.* Hillsdale, NJ: Erlbaum.

Semantic Feature Analysis (Word Matrix)

Social Studies-Forms of Government

	Holds Elections	Government Run by a King or Queen	Government by the People	Government Run by One Person Who Claims Absolute Power	Believes in Capital-ism— Private Ownership of Businesses	Believes that Business and Industry be Owned by the People for the Good of the People	Only One Person Makes Decisions About Business and Industry
Monarchy	−	+	−	+	−	−	?
Democracy	+	−	+	−	+	+	−
Dictatorship	−	−	−	+	−	−	+
Socialist	+	−	?	−	?	+	?

Key: + if yes   − if no   ? if not sure

Anders, P., & Bos, C. (1986). Semantic feature analysis: An interactive strategy for vocabulary development and text comprehension. *Journal of Reading, 29*(7), 610–616.

Possible Sentences

Possible Sentences (Moore & Moore, 1986) combines a vocabulary study with a prediction activity to acquaint students with new vocabulary in the text to be read, support them as they verify the accuracy of the possible statements they create, and generate curiosity for the text to be read. Possible sentences can be used for narrative and expository texts and is most effective when unfamiliar words are mixed with familiar vocabulary.

Five steps are followed in the possible sentence activity:

1. **List key vocabulary words from the text** [The teacher selects key vocabulary terms from the content area textbook or narrative piece. Approximately 6–8 for beginning or striving readers; 10-15 for average and proficient readers. These terms should reflect the key concepts of the text or vocabulary knowledge needed to support comprehension.]
2. **Elicit sentences from students** [Display the words on the chalkboard, chart paper, or overhead. Ask students to pronounce each word after the teacher.]
3. **Read the text to verify generated sentences** [Ask students to compose a sentence that they think could possibly be found in the text for each word. Stress that the sentences must not be personal in nature. In other words, students should avoid sentences such as "I use a *compass* when I go hiking." Rather, the sentences should reflect the type of sentences they would find in a textbook, if expository, or in a narrative story. Write each sentence exactly as dictated by the students, even though they may be inaccurate. Continue with the process until the students are not able to generate any more sentences.]
4. **Evaluate the sentences** [Ask students to read the assigned selection using the generated sentences as their guides. They read to either confirm or refute the information included in their possible sentences. On a sheet numbered from 1–8 or 1–15 (depending on how many sentences were generated), students write a 'T' next to any generated sentences that they believe are **true**, an 'F' next to any generated sentences that they think are **false**, and a 'DK' next to those they are not sure whether they are true or false.]
5. **Create new sentences** [As a whole class or in small groups, have students revise the generated sentences to reflect the way the vocabulary words were used in the text that was read. In other words, students rewrite the sentences to make them true, reflecting how the words were used in the text.]

**A sample possible sentence format may look like this . . .

1. **Key concepts/vocabulary word list**
   compass
   luminous
   breakers
2. **Student-generated possible sentences (before reading) and student-reactions (after reading)**
   T (True), F (False), DK (Don't Know)
   __T__ 1. The scout master used a compass to find his way through the forest.
   __T__ 2. The moonlight was so luminous the soldiers could see their way at night.
   __F__ 3. The breakers in the fuse box need to be switched so the power can be turned on.
3. **Modified sentences (after reading)**
   1. _____
   2. _____
   3. He liked the waves and the rolling breakers as they crashed ashore on the beach.

Moore, D. W., Readence, J. E., & Rickelman, R. J. (1989). *Prereading activities for content area reading and learning.* (2nd ed.). Newark, DE: IRA.

Contextual Redefinition

Contextual Redefinition is an excellent technique for reviewing and integrating word analysis strategies. This technique aids students in the use of context clues by contrasting definitions from words in isolation and words in context (Tierney & Readence, 2000). It provides reinforcement for dictionary skills. It is effective, yet easy to implement. It consists of four steps:

1. **Choosing difficult words**
   - Words are chosen that are important to an understanding of the selection and which may pose problems for students.
2. **Presenting words in isolation**
   - Unfamiliar words are listed on the chalkboard or transparency. Volunteers are invited to pronounce them—they are given help if needed—and are asked to define the words. Because the words are presented in isolation, students must rely on morphemic analysis clues to define the words. Students provide reasons for their definitions; however, because they have little to go on, their proposed definitions may be quite off the mark. Encourage students to agree on one meaning for each word.

     Example word: *vivacious*
3. **Presenting words in context**
   - Words are then presented in context. Ideally, this would be the context in which the words are used in the selection to be read: "*In contrast to her more serious husband, Mary Todd Lincoln was a vivacious and colorful addition to the Washington scene*" (Burchard, 1999, p.49). However, if the context is not adequate, create your own sentence. Using the context, students, in pairs or groups, make their best guesses about the meaning of each word. They are expected to explain why they constructed a particular meaning. This gives them opportunity to share their reasoning processes. The group again must agree on one meaning for each word.
4. **Checking the meaning in the dictionary**
   - Students look up the word in the dictionary and discuss possible definitions with the group. The group chooses the most appropriate definition.
   - **Example:** In deriving the meaning of **vivacious,** students use their knowledge of the root **viv** [life] and the suffix **ous** [full of], the context clue, and the dictionary definition to construct a meaning of the word, *full of life*.

Contextual Redefinition provides a natural way to provide guided practice in three interrelated word identification skills: **morphemic analysis, contextual analysis, and dictionary usage. The procedure helps students to arrive at a fuller, more precise understanding of words.

From: Moore, D. W., Readence, J. E., & Rickelman, R. J. (1989). *Prereading activities for content area reading and learning.* Newark, DE: International Reading Association.

Analogies

Analogies are important for vocabulary development because they help children see relationships between words. Analogies help develop students' cognitive reasoning skills while they make connections with vocabulary words. They are also found in many standardized tests.

There are different types of analogies:

1. **part to whole** [clutch: transmission:: key: _____] (starter, engine, exhaust)
2. **person to situation** [Lincoln: slavery:: _____: independence] (Jefferson, Kennedy, Jackson)
3. **cause and effect** [CB: radio reception:: television: _____] (eating, homework, gym)
4. **synonym** [bourgeoisie: middle class:: proletariat: _____] (upper class, lower class, royalty)
5. **antonym** [pinch: handful:: sip: _____] (pet, gulp, taste)
6. **geography** [Everest: Matterhorn:: _____: Alps] (Ozarks, Andes, Himalayas)
7. **measurement** [minutes: clock:: _____: temperature] (liters, degrees, gradations)
8. **time** [24 hours: rotation:: 365 days: _____] (Eastern time, revolution, axis)

Vacca, R. T., & Vacca, J. L. (1996). *Content area reading.* (5th ed.). New York, NY: HarperCollins.

The example below is a format that can be used for primary grade students that shows the use of words instead of using the single colon (meaning "is to") and double colon (meaning "as"). Once children have become familiar with analogies, the words "is to" and "as" should be replaced with the colon and double colon. After children have become experienced in doing analogies, answer choices can be eliminated in order to provide opportunities for children to come up with their own answers without the use of prompts.

1. Hot **is to** cold **as** day **is to** _____ .
   up   night   long

2. Dog **is to** cat **as** small **is to** _____ .
   little   big   short

3. Puppy **is to** _____ **as** young **is to** old.
   playful   dog   kitten

4. _____ **is to** white **as** on **is to** off.
   Red   Black   Door

5. Happy **is to** _____ **as** stop **is to** go.
   glad   sad   frown

6. Slow **is to** _____ **as** long **is to** short.
   silly   happy   fast

Richardson, J. S., Morgan, R. F., & Fleener, C. (2006). *Reading to learn in the content areas.* Belmont, CA: Thomson Wadsworth Publishing.

Snyder Word Analysis Map (SWAM)

According to Beck, McKeown, and Omanson (1987), students need multiple exposures to new words in order to learn their meanings at an in-depth level. As a college instructor of a developmental reading class, I utilized a variety of ways to help students learn new vocabulary. One of those methods was Schwartz's Concept of Definition Map (1988). The design of this map was beneficial, and I saw my students' success with learning conceptual terms using the Concept of Definition Map. I realized that this graphic organizer did not work as well with all words, especially those that did not concretely represent concepts. Therefore, I developed the **Snyder Word Analysis Map (SWAM)** in 1998 using a modified design of the Schwartz map. The SWAM helps students attack word meanings through morphemic analysis, contextual analysis, and basic elements of word knowledge that can be derived from dictionaries and thesauri. I used the SWAM as one of several ways to expose my fourth graders to learning vocabulary in all subject areas, and they successfully learned the words at a more in-depth level as a result of completing the SWAM.

First, students write a short dictionary definition. Then they analyze the word by determining how many syllables it has and what part of speech it is, based on how the word is used in the text from which it came. Students determine if the word contains any prefixes and/or suffixes and if so, what their meanings are. In addition, they consider whether the word has a root and if so, the origin and meaning of that root. The student provides three synonyms for the word in the same part of speech as the target word and one antonym in the same part of speech. Finally, students write a sentence using the word with good context clues.

Students learn to create a "skeleton" map of the SWAM by thinking of it like a clock. They initially write the target word in the middle. Then at 12:00, they write a short definition. At 2:00, 3:00, 4:00, they write the components of morphemic analysis for the word as indicated in the above paragraph. At 5:00, 6:00, and 7:00, they write three synonyms. At 9:00 they write an antonym, and at 11:00, they write a sentence using good context clues and they underline the target word. After completing the SWAM, a student comes away with a more in-depth understanding of the word and is able to formulate a good definition along with an example sentence.

The target word on the SWAM may be illustrated. It may be drawn by the student or cut and pasted to the page. Students can develop a SWAM based on assigned vocabulary words and present the SWAM after the teacher checks their work. Thus, the student's knowledge of the word is developed even further. See the examples on the following pages.

Beck, I. L., McKeown, M. G., & Omanson, R. C. (1987). The effects and uses of diverse vocabulary instructional techniques. In M. G. McKeown & M. E. Curtis (Eds.). *The nature of vocabulary acquisition* (pp. 147-163). Hillsdale, NJ: Erlbaum.

Schwartz, R. (1988). Learning to learn vocabulary in content area textbooks. *Journal of Reading, 32,* 108-118.

Snyder, A. F. (2009). *Research-based strategies for literacy instruction in grades 3–5.* Dubuque, IA: Kendall-Hunt.

Snyder Word Analysis Map (SWAM), Adapted from Schwartz

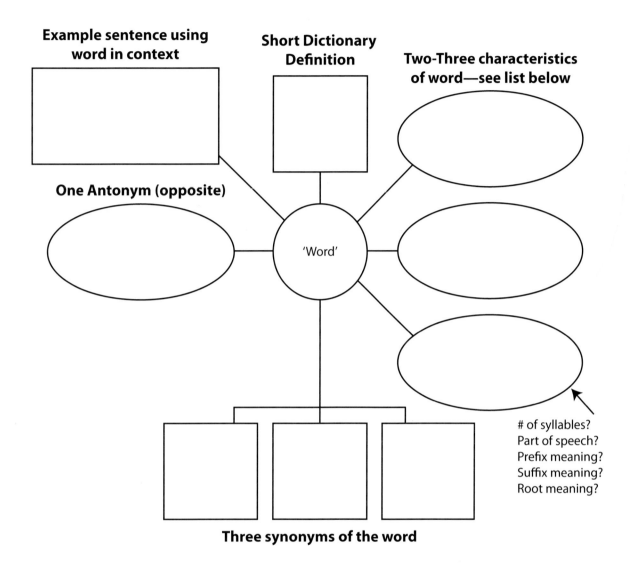

Example sentence using word in context

Short Dictionary Definition

Two-Three characteristics of word—see list below

One Antonym (opposite)

'Word'

# of syllables?
Part of speech?
Prefix meaning?
Suffix meaning?
Root meaning?

Three synonyms of the word

Design of graphic organizer adapted by Alice F. Snyder, 1998, from Robert Schwartz Concept of Definition Map, 1988.

Snyder Word Analysis Map (SWAM)

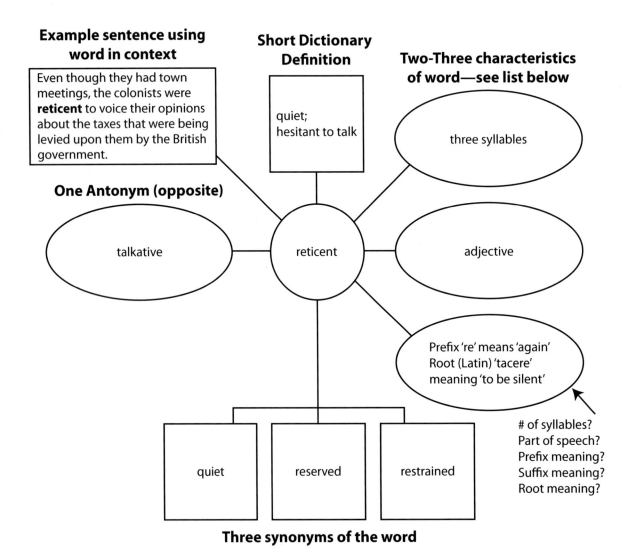

Example sentence using word in context

Even though they had town meetings, the colonists were **reticent** to voice their opinions about the taxes that were being levied upon them by the British government.

Short Dictionary Definition

quiet; hesitant to talk

Two-Three characteristics of word—see list below

three syllables

One Antonym (opposite)

talkative

reticent

adjective

Prefix 're' means 'again' Root (Latin) 'tacere' meaning 'to be silent'

quiet

reserved

restrained

Three synonyms of the word

# of syllables? Part of speech? Prefix meaning? Suffix meaning? Root meaning?

Word Tree Posters

Word Tree Posters help students in grades 4 and up who are at the Derivational Relations stage of spelling development (Bear et al., 2000) to learn root words and their meanings. A Word Tree Poster can be created to last throughout the school year. The teacher creates a large tree to keep on the wall. Materials needed are Velcro, word cards, and sentence strips. Each week, assign a student a new root to investigate. The student goes through steps 3, 4, and 6, placing the root meaning at the base of the tree and words with their definitions on the branches. Additional words students learn throughout the week can be added.

The procedures are as follows:

1. Select a root.
2. Share with each other as many word forms of this root as possible.
3. Use the dictionary and the suffixes and prefixes you know to find new words that you did not think of before.
4. Write the words and a short definition for each using the meaning of the root in your definitions.
5. Draw an outline of a tree.
6. Write the root at the base of the tree and each new word and its definition on individual branches.

A Sample Word Tree Poster for the Latin Root 'dic' and a list of possible high-frequency roots:

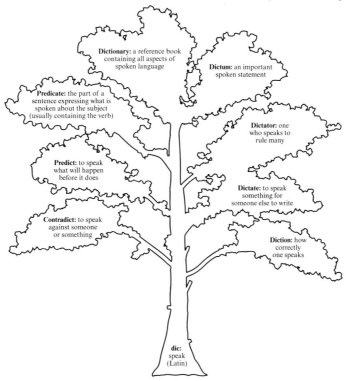

spec [Latin-see]
graph [Greek-write]
rupt [Latin-break]
dic [Latin-speak]
ped [Latin-foot]
loc [Latin-place]
cycl [Greek-circle, ring]

port [Latin-carry]
man [Latin-hand]
script [Latin-write]
vid [Latin-see]
gram [Greek-letter, write]
phon [Greek-sound]
aud [Latin-hear]

cred [Latin-believe]
photo [Greek-light]
tract [Latin-pull, drag]
fac [Latin-make, do]
therm [Greek-heat]
mot [Latin-move]

Adapted from: Bear, D., Invernizzi, M., Templeton, S., & Johnson, F. (2000). *Words their way.* (2nd Ed.). Upper Saddle River, NJ: Prentice Hall.

Vocabulary Self-Selection (VSS) Chart

VSS charts help students "collect" vocabulary words that may pose a problem for them as they read narrative and expository texts. It is essential that with the VSS chart, **students select** the words that they do not know or words they want to learn. The teacher does not pre-select the words. The charts can focus on one specific book, on one particular chapter in a textbook, or the chart can be used as children read and work from a variety of sources. For example, the VSS below is focused on the book *Amos and Boris* (1971) by William Steig. A child may collect words and complete the chart as a before, during, or after reading activity.

Word	Word Parts	Meaning of Word Part(s)	Definition of the Word	Sentence with the Word
telescope	tele	tele- distant; far off	Instrument used to make far away things look closer	Amos used a telescope to see things that were far off in the distance.
luminous	lumin ous	lumin- light ous- full of	Full of light	The ocean looked luminous from the moonlight.

The example below is one that may be used as children select words from multiple texts.

Word	Book	Word Parts	Meaning of Word Parts	Definition of the Word	Sentence with the Word
telescope	Amos and Boris	tele	Distant; far off	Instrument used to make far away things look closer	Amos used a telescope to see things far off in the distance.
metamorphosis	Science	meta morph sis	meta-after morph-change, shape sis-the act of	A change in form or shape	Caterpillars go through metamorphosis as they change into a butterfly.

Adapted from: Haggard, M. R. (1986). The vocabulary self-selection strategy: Using student interest and word knowledge to enhance vocabulary growth. *Journal of Reading, 29* (7), 634–642.

Instructional Strategies for
Comprehension in the Content Areas

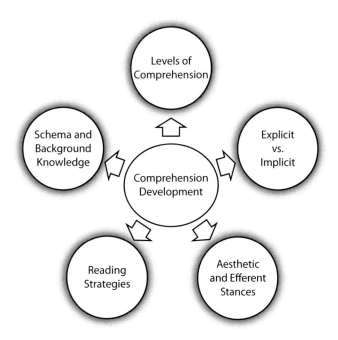

Chapter Two presents a variety of comprehension strategies that teachers may utilize to promote active engagement in constructing meaning in all content areas. They help students interact with informational text in a strategic manner which leads to more efficient learning from text. Literacy and cognitive researchers such as Richard Anderson and P. David Pearson (1984), Palinscar and Brown (1984), and Isabel Beck and Margaret McKeown (2006) have greatly influenced literacy instruction for effective comprehension for decades. These influential researchers have shaped literacy research and instruction for all learners. The strategies in this chapter help students to become critical readers who are able to strategically analyze text in order to learn more effectively. Thus, they not only know what they have read, but they realize the importance of the author's message and its potential significance in their lives. These strategies impact student achievement by helping students to become independent readers and consumers of multiple forms of print, and writers who think creatively and analytically.

The Four Cueing Systems

The four cueing systems provide the inside story to help teachers more effectively understand the ways children approach the process of reading a text. Proficient readers utilize all of these cueing systems because one system informs the other throughout the reading process. Readers apply each of these cueing systems simultaneously as they synthesize the components of the reading process while constructing meaning. The four cueing systems described below lead to the ultimate goal of reading, which is comprehension. All four cueing systems play a critical role for twenty-first century readers as they explore multiple texts in all content areas.

The **grapho-phonic cueing system** relates to the phonological, or sound, system of the English language consisting of 44 sounds, or phonemes, and over 500 ways to spell these 44 sounds. In the elementary grades, instruction in the grapho-phonic cueing system usually involves (a) teaching word pronunciations, (b) noticing rhyming words, (c) decoding words when reading, (d) using invented spelling when writing, (e) detecting regional and other dialects, (f) reading and writing alliterations and onomatopoeia, and (g) syllabication.

Terminology for the Grapho-phonic Cueing System

phonemic awareness—the understanding that speech is made up of individual sounds	phonics—teaching sound-symbol correspondences and spelling "generalizations"	phoneme—the smallest unit of sound	grapheme—a written representation of a phoneme using one or more letters
■ hearing sounds that rhyme (h*at*, s*at*, c*at*, f*at*), alliteration (*S*illy *S*usie *s*aw a *s*eashell.)	■ onsets (b in boat; st in stop) ■ rimes (oat in boat; op in stop) ■ blending and isolating sounds (c-a-t is cat; cat is c-a-t)	/b/ as in boat /ŏ/ as in cot	/ă/ as in cat /ī/ as in bright

The **syntactic cueing system** is the structural system of the English language which governs how words are put together to form sentences. Syntax includes parts of speech and sentence structure. In the elementary grades, instruction in the syntactic cueing system usually involves (a) teaching parts of speech, (b) adding inflectional endings to words, (c) joining words to make compound words, (d) using capitalization and punctuation to designate beginnings and ends of sentences, (e) verb usage, (f) writing simple, compound, and complex sentences, and (g) combining sentences.

Terminology for the Syntactic Cueing System

Syntax	Inflectional Endings (affixes)	Parts of Speech
■ sentence structure and grammar (parts of speech, parts of a sentence, usage, sentence construction, types of sentences)	■ a change in the form of a word by number, gender, case, and tense to indicate certain grammatical relationships	■ eight categories of words based on their syntactic functions
subject, verb, predicate, phrase, independent clause, dependent clause, direct/indirect objects	ing, ed, d, ies, es, s, ly	noun, verb, adjective, adverb, pronoun, preposition, conjunction, interjection

The **semantic cueing system** is the meaning system of language, which focuses on vocabulary as well as understanding the author's message. The ability to comprehend word meanings and the overall message of a text is the ultimate goal of reading. In the elementary grades, instruction in the semantic cueing system usually involves (a) learning multiple meanings of words in a variety of contexts, (b) learning meanings of words from specific disciplines, (c) using context clues to determine meanings of unfamiliar words, (d) learning meanings of prefixes, suffixes, and roots to help determine word meanings, (e) using the dictionary and thesaurus, (f) learning various strategies for literal, interpretive, and critical comprehension, (g) reading and writing comparisons (metaphors, similes), and (h) reading and writing figures of speech.

Terminology for the Semantic Cueing System

Morpheme	Automaticity	Figure of Speech	Context Clue
■ smallest unit of meaning ■ **prefix**—comes in front of a root or base word (un, pre, bi) ■ **suffix**—comes at the end of a root or base word (ness, ment, ish) ■ **root** (chron, lum, vid) (A root word cannot stand alone while a base word can stand by itself.)	■ the ability to identify a word and immediately assign an appropriate meaning to it	■ words used as adjectives or adverbs that create comparisons or descriptions, using colorful, visual terms or phrases ■ simile, metaphor, personification, hyperbole, idiom, onomatopoeia, oxymoron	■ types of indicators a writer uses to help a reader derive meaning without having to use a dictionary; examples, appositives, synonyms, antonyms, usage indicators, schema-based indicators, definition/explanation

Figures of Speech

Figures of Speech	Examples
simile—a comparison of two unlike things using 'like' or 'as'	The shooting stars were like diamonds glittering in the night sky. During the job interview, Susan was as cool as a cucumber because she was well prepared!
metaphor—a comparison of two or more things without using 'like' or 'as'	After Mary shared the good news, Bob's heart overflowed with joy! The fog silently crept in from the ocean and blanketed the tiny village.
personification—using the qualities of a person to describe inanimate objects	The ocean waves whipped the boat as the storm continued to build. The shooting stars danced across the moonlit sky during the meteor shower.
hyperbole—words that exaggerate	I am so hungry I could eat a horse! I have a million things to do! I had a ton of homework!
idiom—expressions that have unique meanings that do not align with the literal meanings of the words or phrases	Be sure to wear your coat or you will catch cold. Eat your heart out because our team will surely win this game!
onomatopoeia—words that resemble the sounds to which they refer	beep; ding dong
oxymoron—use of words with contradictory or clashing ideas next to one another	accidentally on purpose; original copy; working vacation; random order; deafening silence

Context Clues

Note that the vocabulary word is underlined while the context clues are italicized in bold print.

Context Clues	Examples
example—using the words 'such as' or 'for example' to designate specific details to clarify a word's meaning	The moonlight was so *bright that we did not need a flashlight* to illuminate the path as we hiked toward the dining hall. Hoofed mammals include animals from the equine group, *such as horses and zebras.*
appositives—using commas to separate an immediate renaming of the word with a definition or more simplistic terminology	During a field trip to the aquarium, the children saw a rookery, *or group,* of penguins swimming playfully in the pool. Matthew the Pilgrim took his blunderbuss, *or gun,* to hunt for a wild turkey for the harvest feast.
synonyms—extending understanding by using a word with the same meaning	A tiara with 100 diamonds was used as the *crown* for the 2011 Homecoming Queen during the parade. Father had to shop at the haberdashery to find a new *suit, tie, and shoes* for Jim's graduation.
antonyms—clarifying meaning by using a word that means the opposite	When the children found out that they would be spending vacation at Disneyworld rather than at the Civil War museum, they became *joyful rather than* dejected.
usage indicators—identifying the purpose and function of the word in the sentence	The crane *lifted* the huge drainage pipe and placed it in the ditch. The cheerleaders used megaphones to *increase the loudness* of their voices as they cheered for the team.
schema-based indicators—using one's prior knowledge or experience to clarify a word's meaning	As Jane recalled *memories of taking college placement exams* during her senior year in high school, she understood her daughter's feelings of dread as she left that morning to take the SATs. Jane knew that Susan's *test scores would have an impact on whether she would be accepted at Harvard.*
definition/explanation—providing a definition or explanation immediately after the word is used	Dr. Martin is a geologist, *or an expert on rocks and minerals.* The driver was traveling *so fast* that he *lost control* as the car veered off the road, *went down an embankment, and hit a tree.*

The **pragmatic cueing system** refers to the usage and function of language in social and cultural contexts. Pragmatics relates to the purpose for using language in both standard English and nonstandard English. Standard English is used in textbooks, academia, and by media, such as TV news. Nonstandard English refers to other forms of language, such as slang, colloquialisms, and dialectical variations. In the elementary grades, instruction in the pragmatic cueing system involves (a) comparing standard and non-standard English, (b) dialogues using various dialects in reading and writing activities, (c) modifying language to fit designated purposes, and (d) teaching students how to establish a purpose for reading.

Terminology for the Pragmatic Cueing System

stance—purpose for reading **aesthetic stance**—reading for pleasure or making an emotional connection with the text **efferent stance**—reading to learn and to gain information	**dialect**—a form of language distinctive to a group or region that differs from the standard language in pronunciation, syntax, and semantics	**colloquialism**—informal speech and writing designating a particular region

Flint, A. S. (2008). *Literate lives: Teaching reading & writing in elementary classrooms.* Hoboken, NJ: John Wiley & Sons, Inc.

Levels of Comprehension

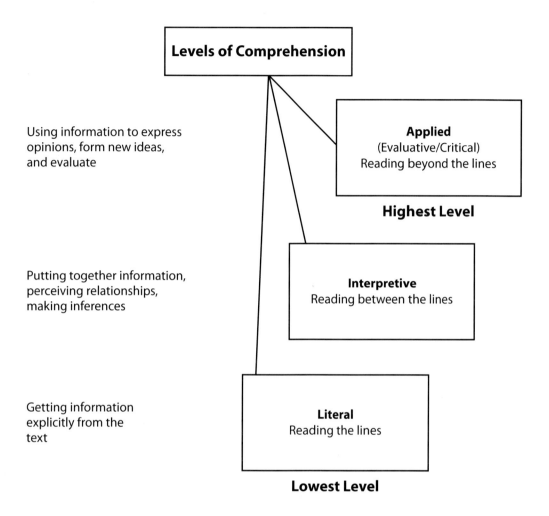

As teachers prepare lessons on comprehension skills and strategies, they must be cognizant of the three levels of comprehension shown in the graphic above. It is important to consider this framework in order to ensure that comprehension instruction extends to higher levels of thought as children become critical consumers of content area texts. The next page lists the various strategies and skills associated with each of the three levels of comprehension. Chapter Two provides a variety of strategies for exploring various levels of comprehension that help support students' metacognitive development as they become strong comprehenders of informational texts.

Adapted from: Vacca, R. T., & Vacca, J. L. (1996). *Content area reading.* (5th ed.). New York, NY: HarperCollins College Publishers.

Literacy Comprehension Skills and Strategies

Skills and Strategies of Literal Comprehension (Level 1)

- Recalling **explicit** details—who, what, when, where
- Following written directions
- Recalling **explicit** sequence of events
- Identifying **stated** cause-effect relationships
- Comparing and contrasting information
- Identifying **stated** topic and main idea
- Identifying **stated** character traits and actions
- Understanding symbols, abbreviations, and acronyms—translating abbreviated forms of words into meaningful units
- Reading for a **stated** purpose—determining information to be learned from the reading; formulate this information into questions; read to answer the questions

Skills and Strategies of Interpretive Comprehension (Level 2)

- Predicting outcomes—relating elements within a passage to each other in order to determine the result
- Determining **implied** main idea—unstated main topic, idea, theme, or message
- Selecting **implied** cause-effect relationships—interpreting from stated information the implied relationships in an event
- Identifying an **implied** sequence of events—inferring from given information the order of ideas or information
- Interpreting figurative language
- Making inferences schema-based—depends on BK; text-based—putting together 2+ bits of information from text
- Understanding mood and emotional reactions—responding to imagery or feeling conveyed by the author
- Summarizing information—condensing the information read
- Making generalizations—apply reasoning to given facts in order to make a decision
- Perceiving relationships—identify similarities among ideas in a passage and relate or classify the ideas
- Making connections—Text-to-Text; Text-to-Self; Text-to-World

Skills and Strategies of Applied/Evaluative/Critical Comprehension (Level 3)

- Differentiating between facts and opinions
- Interpreting propaganda techniques—identifying ideas or doctrines promoted by a special group
- Using problem-solving techniques
- Recognizing fallacies in reasoning—recognizing words used to create an illusion, causing illogical or unsound ideas to be relayed
- Identifying relevant and irrelevant information
- Determining reliability of the author
- Evaluating ideas and concepts across texts
- Applying what has been learned to the reader's own purposes—seeing the relationship of what is read to one's own situation and determine possible application
- Evaluating character's actions—judge or evaluate information based on theories, etc.—make moral decisions, judgments
- Placing self in character's shoes and evaluate—i.e., "If you were Brian, would you have . . . ? Why or why not?" or "If you were General Lee . . ." or "Given what you know about Robert E. Lee, would you have chosen to fight for the South or the North? Why or why not?"

Background Knowledge: Prior Knowledge and Making Connections

Proficient readers activate background knowledge (BK or PK) and make personal connections to text automatically. Inexperienced or struggling readers must be explicitly taught to make connections by using texts that they can link to their own experiences. For students who may have limited background experiences or who may have trouble making connections to their own lives, the teacher must design experiences for them and then model, through think-alouds, how connections can be made. There are three types of connections:

Text to Self (T-S)—the child connects the text to his/her own personal experiences

Text to Text (T-T)—the child connects the text to another text he/she has read or viewed

Text to World (T-W)—the child connects the text with his/her own general knowledge about the world and how things "work" in the world around him

An introductory lesson on making connections using background knowledge

Materials—Any picture book you have a personal connection with and can use to make connections with other texts or connections with general knowledge about the world; post-it notes, pens & pencils, the board. [You can also choose books that focus on only one type of connection at a time. For example, a book that you and the students can only make Text-to-Self connections for one lesson, then focus a different lesson on a text that you and the students can make Text-to-Text connections, etc.]

Setting the Stage—Ask the students to tell you what **Background Knowledge** means. After a brief discussion, explain what it means and give examples. Introduce the book by sharing with them that the book reminds you of your childhood, family, etc. Briefly discuss the story's plot.

Shared Reading—Read the book aloud to the students. As you read, think aloud about how certain parts of the book remind you of something. Demonstrate how to write notes on the post-it notes as you remember things. Once the students seem to understand and offer their own connections, give them a post-it note to write their own connections, making sure they put their names on the post-its. Encourage them to make connections for the rest of the book.

Conclusion and Follow-up—Go back and reread the connections that were made. Re-emphasize why it is important to make connections while reading. After introducing the three types of connections, go back to the connections made during this lesson and label each with what type of connection it is, T-T, T-S, and T-W. Place them on the three-column **Making Connections Chart** (see next page).

Adapted from handout materials from 2001 workshop based on: Harvey, S., & Goudvis, A. (2000). *Strategies that work: Teaching comprehension to enhance understanding*. York, ME: Stenhouse.

Making Connections Chart

On the chart below, record the connections that you make while you read using the correct note pattern.

Text-to-Text

Text-to-Self

Text-to-World

Background Knowledge Activity

Three Sisters

Readers are often presented with texts that they may consider somewhat ambiguous based on the amount of background knowledge they bring to a particular reading task. As a result, they must rely on their prior knowledge and experiences to make inferences as they construct meaning from these reading assignments. As an exercise, use your background knowledge as you read the poem and answer the questions below.

Three Sisters

With hocked gems financing him
Our hero bravely defied all scornful laughter
That tried to prevent his scheme.

Your eyes deceive, he said;
An egg, not a table
Correctly typifies this unexpected domain.

Now three sturdy sisters sought proof
Forging along sometimes through calm vastness
Yet more often over turbulent peaks and valleys.

Days became weeks
As many doubters spread
Fearful rumors about the edge.

At last from nowhere
Welcome winged creatures appeared
Signifying momentous success.

Now, answer the questions below:

1. What was hocked?
2. How many sisters were there?
3. How long were they gone?
4. Who or what appeared at the end of the poem?
5. Find three describing words. _____, _____, _____
6. Who was the implied main character in the poem?
7. From your own knowledge base, what do you know about him?

Where in the poem did you achieve comprehension? How?

Poem from: Ornstein, R. (1991). *Evolution of consciousness.* New York, NY: Simon and Schuster.

Activating Background Knowledge

One of the most important facets of instruction involving reading in the content areas is activating or building background knowledge prior to reading. Children enter the learning process with a myriad of prior experiences that provide a range of background knowledge that may or may not assist them as they read a variety of texts. The scenarios below demonstrate ineffective and effective ways for activating background knowledge prior to reading.

Ineffective Way to Activate Prior Knowledge

"Today we are going to read the article 'Birds in Winter.' How many of you have ever seen birds during the winter?" (Student Response) "What are the types of birds that you typically see in the winter months?" (SR) "How do birds get their food in wintertime?" (SR)

Effective Way to Activate Prior Knowledge (Schema Directed)

"Today we are going to read the article 'Birds in Winter.' Before we read it, I would like you to think about some key ideas that will help you understand what you're about to read. From the title, what do you think this article is going to be about?" (Record SRs & discuss). "Yes, this article talks about what birds do to survive during a blizzard." (Write the word *blizzard* on the board. Connect the students' predictions to surviving in a blizzard.)

"What is a blizzard?" (SR. Write a sentence on the board using the word *blizzard*, and discuss its meaning.) "What do you think it means to survive in a blizzard? What possible problems might birds have surviving during a blizzard?" (Discuss questions; list students' answers on the board, and discuss them. Add your own points to the discussion to extend and clarify.) "How might surviving in a blizzard be different for birds than surviving in a hurricane?"

Example responses:

1. A blizzard is a terrible snowstorm with very high winds.
2. Birds could have many problems surviving in a blizzard, such as getting food, not freezing to death, finding water to drink, finding a place to sleep that is protected from the wind. Surviving a hurricane doesn't involve the freezing temperatures, with rain instead of snow, although the wind is still strong. Finding food may not be as difficult for birds with a hurricane.

(Adapted from workshop materials, 2001)

Inferential Meaning

Inferring meaning is the foundation of comprehension. We make inferences all the time. Inferring is about reading facial expressions, body language, voice tone, as well as reading "between the lines" of written text. One basic, introductory lesson in making inferences involves helping children understand their own and others' feelings by responding to verbal clues. In a higher-level lesson, students may make inferences from facts or quotes in the text. As with other comprehension skills and strategies, students must be explicitly taught to make inferences. They must be given multiple opportunities to practice the skill with a variety of texts during guided reading or whole class discussion of content area reading. As students become more proficient with the skill, they may practice independently or while engaging in literature circle groups. Some texts that could be used to develop inferential meaning are: *Dandelions* by Eve Bunting, *Rose Blanche* by Christophe Gallaz, *Tight Times* by Barbara Shook Hazen, and *Teammates* by Peter Golenbock.

Introductory Inferring Lesson

Purpose: To help students better understand their own feelings and to introduce inferential thinking.

Resources: Large index cards with feeling words written on them. (One card is pinned or taped on the back of one student volunteer who doesn't know what it says.)

Procedure: After discussing feelings, the teacher chooses one feeling word and tapes it to the student volunteer's back. Other students form a large circle around the student volunteer. Student volunteer slowly turns around so that the others can see the word. The teacher asks the class to give clues for the word by starting with "I felt that way when…" For example, for the word **frustrated**, the students might give clues like:

- I felt that way when the computer shut down in the middle of my project and I lost all of my work.
- I felt that way when I could not solve a puzzle.

After four or five students have a chance to give a clue, the teacher asks the volunteer if he/she can infer what the feeling may be. If the student answers correctly, the teacher asks the volunteer how he/she made the inference without actually hearing the word. If the volunteer answers incorrectly, others continue with clues until the volunteer answers correctly or the teacher provides assistance. The game continues with a few more student volunteers and new feeling words are used.

Adapted from: Harvey, S., & Goudvis, A. (2000). *Strategies that work.* York, ME: Stenhouse. (pgs. 105–106).

Inferential Thinking While Reading

(Two Examples of Recording Sheets)

As you read, mark a sentence or picture with an 'X' when you make an inference. Then copy the sentence or describe (in your own words) the picture from which you made the inference. Then record your inference below.

Name _____   Date _____

Quote or Picture from the Text	Inference Made

(For expository texts...)

Name _____   Date _____

Facts Taken from the Text	Inference Made

Adapted from S. Harvey, S. & Goudvis, A. (2000). *Strategies that work.* York: ME: Stenhouse. [p.278]

Concept Attainment

Concept Attainment is an inquiry-based activity suited for grades 1–5 that takes place prior to beginning a new book or when introducing a new topic or theme to be studied in one of the content areas. Based on the work of Jerome Bruner, concept attainment helps learners develop understandings about conceptual knowledge by finding commonalities among ideas and concepts. It can be done as an individual, partner, or small group activity, although it works best when done in partners. The teacher determines what overlying theme or topic is being presented in the upcoming text.

First, compose about six example sentences that depict the theme or topic in a variety of contexts and about four non-example sentences that do not depict the theme or topic. (Depending on the age of the students, pictures or objects may be used in place of sentences.). Cut out each set of ten sentences and give them to each pair. Give two cards, one with a 'Yes' and one with a 'No,' to each pair of students.

To begin the concept attainment activity, do not give specific directions other than telling the students, *"Read the statements and decide which ones should go under the 'yes' column and which ones should go under the 'no' column, based on what the sentences say."* After giving the students a few minutes to read and ponder over the statements, ask *"Does anyone have a guess as to what one of the 'yes' statements might be?"* Take only one volunteer. The student gives the number of the statement and reads it orally to the class. The teacher then rereads the statement and says *"That's a 'yes' statement,"* **or** *"That's actually a 'no' statement."* *"Now that you have one clue, continue discussing the rest of the statements and see what you think now."*

Give the students a couple more minutes to ponder. Then ask *"Does anyone have a guess as to what another 'yes' statement might be?"* Take one more volunteer's guess and give the appropriate feedback. Then after a couple more minutes, ask, *"Does anyone know what a 'no' statement might be?"* Take one volunteer's possible 'no' statement and give the appropriate feedback. Give a couple more minutes for the students to consider their statements and think about the ways all the 'yes' statements go together. After this, ask the students if anyone can identify what the overarching concept or theme the 'yes' statements have in common. Students give their responses and their reasoning for their responses.

Throughout this discovery-inquiry activity, the teacher does not give clues to the students to help them. This activity is designed to allow students to attain the concept or theme to be studied on their own with peer support. Below is an example of concept attainment statements for the concept of **survival** for grades 4–8. The **Y** and **N** at the end of each statement indicate whether the statement does or does not represent the concept. Of course, critical discussion often takes place when students defend their choices!

1. John studied very hard for his final exams because if his grades didn't improve, he would definitely be drafted and sent to Vietnam. (Y or N)
2. Once their raft drifted onto the shore, the family began to gather anything they could to eat, what they could use to build a shelter, and what they needed to build a fire. (Y)
3. Face to face with the bear, the hiker knew she had to curl up into a ball and play "dead" in hopes the bear would not be threatened and thus, walk away. (Y)
4. The jogger increased the number of miles he ran each day to prepare for the upcoming Boston Marathon. (Y)
5. After his grueling interview, Bob went to his favorite restaurant and ate his favorite comfort foods. (N)
6. The motorist, being trapped in the overturned car for three days, drank rainwater to keep himself from dehydrating. (Y)
7. When he saw that the pilot had a heart attack, Kevin knew he would have to try to land the plane himself. (Y)
8. Frank asked a couple of big football players to escort him to school to protect him from the bullies. (Y)
9. After a long day at the construction site, Sue came home, swam ten laps in her pool, and relaxed in the shade. (N)
10. The mother raccoon fought off the bobcat to protect her babies. (Y)
11. Melinda practiced playing challenging concertos so she could enter the upcoming competition for placement at the Julliard School of Music. (N)

Talking Drawings

Purpose: To help readers use prior knowledge to improve their recall and comprehension of narrative and expository texts. Talking Drawings enhances visual/spatial learners' understanding of ideas, concepts, and information gleaned from reading (Gardner, 1983). This strategy helps readers to create mental images before and after reading as they construct meaning. The Talking Drawings strategy offers readers opportunities to draw what they visualize prior to reading, using their prior knowledge and understanding about the concept or topic. After reading, learners construct other drawings to demonstrate what they have discovered from reading.

Audience: Elementary, middle, and secondary students

Before Reading:

Step One: Tell students to close their eyes and imagine topic X, event X, or character X that will be the focus of the lesson, reading assignment, or activity. After a few seconds, ask them to open their eyes and draw what they see in their minds.

Step Two: Students share their drawings with one or two other students, talking about and analyzing their drawings, explaining why they drew what they did.

Step Three: Students may volunteer to share their drawings with the entire class in which they may share personal experiences and information sources that came into play when they drew their pictures. A concept map may be written on the board that reflects contributions of the class.

During Reading:

Step Four: Students read the assigned textbook pages, sections, articles, or narrative texts, keeping their drawings in mind as they read.

After Reading:

Step Five: After the text has been read, engage the class (or small groups) in discussion of the text, article, or narrative text, asking students to create a new drawing based on new understandings gained from their reading.

Step Six: Students share and/or compare their before and after reading drawings, discussing their changes and reasons for any changes made. They are encouraged to revisit the text to explore specific passages that support their changes.

Step Seven: Students are then encouraged to write about how their before and after drawings have changed and any new understandings they have developed throughout the process.

Step Eight: As an optional step, students may then conduct further research on the topic on the Internet or other sources.

McConnell, S. (1992/1993). Talking drawings: A strategy for assisting learners. *Journal of Reading, 36*(4), 260–269.

Talking Drawings Sample Expository Lesson

1. Close your eyes and think about <u>volcanoes</u>. Now, open your eyes and draw what you saw.

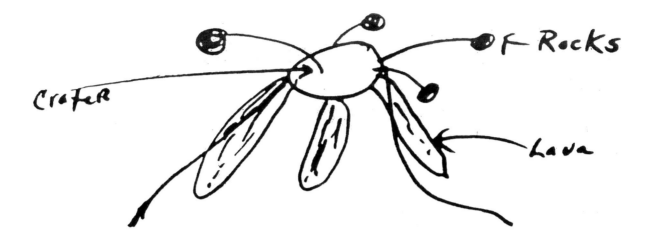

2. Read your selection on "Volcanoes" from Chapter 12 then draw a second picture to show what you learned.

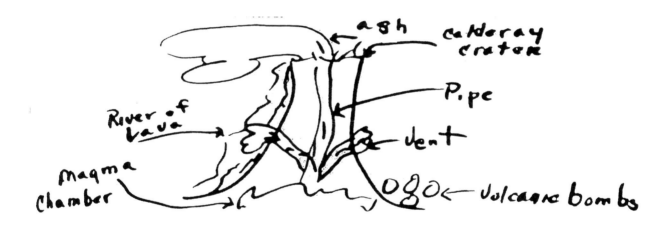

3. In the space below, tell what you have changed about your before and after pictures.

At first, I only drew the mountain and the lava coming down the sides. From our textbook and the video, I learned that there is a magma chamber inside that causes the eruption to flow through the pipe and out the caldera, the huge opening at the top. There is a river of lava that flows down the side of the mountain. Ash and volcanic bombs can be seen around the volcano.

KWL

Purpose: KWL helps determine students' prior knowledge and prior experiences before, during, and after reading to increase their comprehension and recall of expository material. It is a schema-based, brainstorming activity that organizes what students already know, what they want to learn about a topic prior to reading and instruction, and what they learned as a result of reading and instruction. In a standard KWL chart, the "**K**" represents what students already know about the topic, the "**W**" stands for what they **want** to know or learn more about the topic which guides their reading, and "**L**" stands for what they **learned** in the course of reading and instruction.

Audience: Elementary, Middle, and Secondary Students

Before Reading:

Step One: Display the KWL chart on the overhead, on large chart paper, or on the board. Provide an individual KWL chart to each child. Explain what each column represents.

Step Two: Ask students to think about everything they know about the topic the class is going to be studying. As each student provides a response about what he or she knows, write the child's response under the "**K**" column in the child's exact words. In parentheses, write the child's name after the response. In this way, you are conveying that the child's response is worthy of noting. If the response is long, you may ask "If I understand you correctly, are you saying . . .?" If the child agrees, then a shortened version may be written with the child's name placed after the response as indicated. On their own copies of the KWL, students write the responses accordingly.

Step Three: Next, ask students what they would like to learn about the topic. Write these contributions under the "**W**" column, indicating the name of the child who contributed each statement. The teacher may add a couple questions or items and emphasize important concepts. This list of questions highlights purposes for reading to motivate and guide students as they read for information.

During Reading:

Step Four: Tell students to read the assigned text(s), referring to the "**W**" column as a guide. (The KWL works well with multiple texts, such as videos, experiments, lectures, and others.)

After Reading:

Step Five: Once students have read the text, ask them to brainstorm what they learned and write their responses under the "**L**" column of the chart. Remember to write the child's name after each contribution. The teacher may need to prompt for additional key concepts that children may not mention.

From: Ogle, D. S. (1986). K-W-L group instructional strategy. In A. S. Palincsar, D. S. Ogle, B. F. Jones, & E. G. Carr (Eds.), *Teaching reading as thinking* (Teleconference Resource Guide, pp. 11–17). Alexandria, VA: Association for Supervision and Curriculum Development.

KWL Chart

What I (We) Know	What I (We) Want to Know	What I (We) Learned

KWL Plus

Purpose: The KWL-Plus helps determine students' prior knowledge and prior experiences before, during, and after reading to increase their comprehension and recall of expository material. The KWL-Plus is a schema-based, brainstorming activity that assesses what students already know, what they want to learn about a topic prior to reading and instruction, and what they learned as a result of reading and instruction. In addition, it helps them **organize** the learned information. With the **KWL-Plus**, students take the KWL one step further by **categorizing** the information they listed in the "L" column. From there, students are encouraged, with the teacher's assistance, to create a graphic organizer of the categorized information.

Audience: Elementary, Middle, and Secondary Students

Before Reading:

Step One: Display the KWL-Plus chart on the overhead, on large chart paper, or on the board. Provide an individual KWL-Plus chart to each child. Explain what each column represents.

Step Two: Ask students to think about everything they know about the topic the class is going to be studying. As each student provides a response about what he or she knows, write the child's response under the "K" column in the child's exact words. In parentheses, write the child's name after the response. In this way, you are conveying that the child's response is worthy of noting. If the response is long, you may ask "If I understand you correctly, are you saying…?" If the child agrees, then a shortened version may be written with the child's name placed after the response. On their own copies of the chart, students write the responses accordingly.

Step Three: Next, ask the students what they would like to learn about the topic. Write these contributions under the "W" column, indicating the name of the child who contributed each statement. The teacher may add a couple questions or items to help emphasize important concepts. This list of questions highlights purposes for reading to motivate and guide students as they read for information.

During Reading:

Step Four: Tell students to read the assigned text(s), referring to the "W" column as a guide. (The KWL works well with multiple texts, such as videos, experiments, lectures, and others.)

After Reading:

Step Five: Once students have read the text, ask them to brainstorm what they learned and write their responses under the "L" column of the chart. Remember to write the child's name after each contribution. The teacher may need to prompt for additional key concepts that children may not mention.

Step Six: Ask students to think about how they may categorize the information listed in the "**What I learned and still need to know**" column. Guide students in this process by modeling a few examples. You may do this by using letter or pictorial symbols to represent categories, then have students categorize the information accordingly. As a class or in small groups, organize the categories into a **semantic web**.

Writing Stage:

Step Seven: Put students into pre-assigned groups or pairs. Ask them to choose one of the categories and write a paragraph about the information in that category. They may refer to the text if needed. Pairs or groups may share their paragraphs with the class when finished. The teacher may want to model, through the think-aloud process, how to take information on a graphic organizer and convert it to a cohesive paragraph. Overall, this activity is a great way to demonstrate to students how they can read for information, then organize what they learned into a graphic organizer that can assist them in the process of writing a report or other informational forms of writing.

From: Carr, E., & Ogle, D. M. (1987). K-W-L-Plus: A strategy for comprehension and summarization. *Journal of Reading, 30,* 626–631.

KWL Plus

All About Tigers (World Wildlife Fund, 1988)

1. Whole class/small group contributions (steps 2–6)

What I Know	What I Want to Learn	What I Learned and Still Need to Know
▪ They live in jungles (Tim) ▪ They have sharp teeth (Susie) ▪ They look a lot like house cats (Jamila) ▪ They hunt for their food (Roberto)	▪ What animals do they hunt for to eat? (Yung) ▪ How big can tigers get? (Erika) ▪ How do they teach their babies to hunt? (Maria) ▪ What countries in the world do they live? (teacher)	▪ live in jungle forests (Tim) **[L]** ▪ Western India and Southeast Asia (Tim) **[L]** ▪ every tiger has different stripes-none look alike (Jamila) **[A]** ▪ hunt deer, antelopes, wild pigs (John) **[E]** ▪ thick pads on feet to hunt silently (Roberto) **[A]** ▪ mother teaches cubs how to hunt and get along in the jungle (Maria) **[B]** ▪ also eat fish, birds, berries, eggs (Yung) **[E]** ▪ front teeth-fangs-used to bite and tear meat (Susie) **[A]** ▪ male tigers can weigh 700 lbs. & be 10 ft. long (Erika) **[A]** ▪ like to swim when it's hot (Maria) **[B]** ▪ sleep during the day (Tim) **[B]** ▪ hunt at night (Roberto) **[B]** ▪ Stripes hide them in shadows (Jamila) **[A]**

2. Class or Group Created Semantic Map (Step 6)

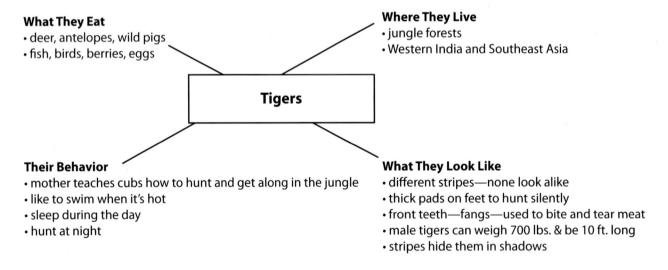

What They Eat
• deer, antelopes, wild pigs
• fish, birds, berries, eggs

Where They Live
• jungle forests
• Western India and Southeast Asia

Tigers

Their Behavior
• mother teaches cubs how to hunt and get along in the jungle
• like to swim when it's hot
• sleep during the day
• hunt at night

What They Look Like
• different stripes—none look alike
• thick pads on feet to hunt silently
• front teeth—fangs—used to bite and tear meat
• male tigers can weigh 700 lbs. & be 10 ft. long
• stripes hide them in shadows

3. Summary for "Appearance/What They Look Like" (Step 7)

Tigers are very large, wild cats. They look like house cats. Male tigers can weigh up to 700 pounds and can measure ten feet long. Just like people, no two tigers look alike. Every tiger has different stripes. These stripes help to hide them in shadows. They have thick pads on their feet that help them hunt quietly. They also have large front teeth called fangs that are used to bite and tear meat.

Reciprocal Questioning (ReQuest)

Reciprocal Questioning (Manzo, 1969) enhances comprehension through a process of back and forth questioning between the teacher and the students. It is based on two major premises: (1) asking the right question is as important as knowing the correct answer, especially when the purpose of reading is to gain information from a text, and (2) the teacher is a powerful model for student behavior. Thus, if students are exposed to an excellent model, such as a teacher who asks good questions about texts, then they will adapt similar questioning strategies and begin to ask good "teacher-type" questions while they read. ReQuest facilitates the learning process, helping students to develop as independent and efficient readers of informational texts. The sequence to the ReQuest procedure is as follows:

1. The teacher assigns a short section of text for students (and teacher) to read silently. Once everyone is finished reading, the teacher turns his/her book over and invites students to ask "teacher-type" questions about the section of text just read. The teacher answers questions as well as possible. Then students turn their books over as the teacher asks any follow-up questions about the same portion of text in order to call attention to other important information in that section. The students answer these follow-up questions.
2. The teacher assigns the next short section of text for everyone to read silently. This time, the teacher turns his/her book over and the students ask questions about that portion of the text that the teacher must attempt to answer.
3. The teacher assigns another short section of text for all to read silently. Students turn their books over once they have finished reading. The teacher asks questions, ensuring that questions tie in to those from the previous segment in order to help students perceive the importance of integration and accumulation of knowledge and ideas. Students answer these questions.
4. The teacher assigns another short section for all to read. This time, the teacher turns book over and students ask questions and the teacher answers them, adding other questions if needed.
5. This procedure continues until students are able to predict what is going to happen, what other information they are going to obtain, or what they need to do to complete activities or exercises. (For example, the teacher might say, "Based on what we have read so far, what do you think will happen in the rest of the chapter?") This procedure may continue until the chapter or lesson in the text is completed.

Categories of Questions for ReQuest Strategy

1. Text-explicit questions—questions can be answered directly from the text.
2. Questions that link to common knowledge or background knowledge and can be reasonably answered ("Based on what you know about . . . what . . .?" "How . . .?" "Where would you . . .?").
3. Questions for which the teacher does not expect a correct answer, but for which the teacher can provide some information ("Have you ever seen a . . .?").
4. Questions that invite the students to ponder about because neither the teacher nor the text is likely to provide a "correct" answer but they are still worth consideration or discussion ("I wonder how . . .?").
5. Questions that can be answered but not from the text being read; further reference is needed in order to answer the question.
6. Questions that require translation, such as from one level of abstraction to another, from one symbolic form or verbal form to another ("In your own words. . . .").

Manzo, A. (1969). The ReQuest Procedure. *Journal of Reading, 13,* 123–126.

Reciprocal Teaching (RT)

Reciprocal Teaching (Palinscar & Brown, 1984) is an excellent student-lead procedure that can be used for narrative and expository texts. This research-based reading and discussion strategy takes place in a small group setting. Through the reciprocal teaching procedure, each group member will serve as a leader who follows a four-step process with a predetermined section of the text. After leading the group through the four steps of the designated section of the text, another group member becomes the leader and he/she proceeds through the four-step process with the next predetermined section of the text, and so on, until the text has been read and each group member has served in the leader role. Below is the four-step sequence that each leader follows as he/she leads the group through the active reading process.

Four Step Sequence Used in Reciprocal Teaching

(This process is repeated for each new section and each new leader.)

Step 1: Prediction: Activate prior knowledge and set purpose for reading. Students then read the section of the text *silently.* (The leader helps group members survey the section and determines the purpose for reading after surveying.)

Step 2: Questioning: Focus on main ideas and check for understanding. (The leader asks questions that pull main idea(s) of the section. The leader asks group members if they have any questions about the reading.) Together, the group constructs meaning.

Step 3: Seeking Clarification: Ensure that readers are actively engaged and check for understanding. (The leader asks group members if there is anything about the section that is still confusing to them.) The group collaboratively clarifies by seeking dictionary support, other resources, revisiting text, etc.

Step 4: Summarization: Require students to pay attention to critical content. (The leader summarizes the section of text that was read and discussed.)

The next section is assigned to a new group leader who begins the process once again with Step 1.

Palinscar, A., & Brown, A. (1984). Reciprocal teaching of comprehension fostering and comprehension monitoring activities. *Cognition and Instruction, 1*(2), 117–175.

Questioning the Author (QtA)

Questioning the Author is a research-based strategy that engages students in an interactive reading experience with the author. With this strategy, students learn to think from an author's perspective based on a set of queries relating to specific goals that the teacher may want readers to explore, depending on the nature of the text. Teachers may use six major modes of interaction during a QtA discussion of narrative or expository texts. Teachers may want to help students become aware of these six modes of interaction and ultimately prepare students to conduct their own QtA discussions in small groups.

Six Modes of Teacher Interaction

Marking—Teacher highlights a student's comment or idea that is important to the meaning being built

> **Example:** "As Susan said, Amos did not think he was going to be able to last very long treading water in the middle of the ocean."

Turning Back—Teacher turns students' attention back to the text to get more information, fix up a misreading, or clarify their thinking

> **Example:** "If you look back on page 8, it says *But it evaded his grasp and went bowling along under full sail, and he never saw it again.* So Amos could not catch up with his boat because the sails were open and the ocean breeze and currents carried it away from him."

Revoicing—Teacher helps students clearly express what they are trying to say

> **Example:** "If I understand you correctly, John, you are saying that even though Amos was upset with Boris for diving underwater without warning Amos, Amos did not stay mad at Boris very long because he knew that Boris saved his life? Is that what you meant?"

Modeling—Teacher shows how he/she may go about creating meaning, how he/she clarifies a difficult passage, draws a conclusion, visualizes a complex process, uses context to determine word meaning

> **Example:** "Hmmm, I'm not sure what the word *sound* means here. I know what a *sound* is, but in this sentence, *From then on, whenever Boris wanted to* **sound***, he warned Amos in advance and got his okay, and whenever he* **sounded***, Amos took a swim.*, the word is used as a verb because of *to sound* and *he sounded.* I know that whales make sounds, but that alone would not make Amos go somersaulting into the water. I can look at the picture and here I see Boris diving into the water and Amos taking a tumble off Boris's back, so maybe when a whale **sounds**, that means he dives into the water. I'll look it up in the dictionary to make sure I'm right."

Annotating—Teacher fills in information that is missing from discussion but is important to understanding key ideas; may be information author left out (inferencing)

> **Example:** "Mice can swim, but they cannot swim for long periods of time."

Recapping—Teacher highlights key points and summarizes

> **Example:** "This story is about a mouse named Amos that loves the ocean so much that he studies navigation and builds a boat that he takes out onto the ocean to explore the world. After falling off his boat, he is saved by a whale named Boris that takes him back to his homeland. After discovering that they are both mammals and spending time together, they became the best of friends. Years later, Boris was washed ashore onto Amos's homeland by a fierce hurricane. Amos tells Boris he will help him, but Boris does not know how a small mouse like Amos can help a huge whale like him. But Amos goes and gets two large elephants that roll Boris back into the water. The two old friends say good-bye, not knowing if they will ever see each other again."

Adapted from: Beck, I. L., McKeown, M. G., Hamilton, R. L., & Kucan, L. (1997). *Questioning the author: An approach for enhancing student engagement with text.* Newark, DE: International Reading Association.
Examples using: Steig, W. (1971). *Amos & Boris.* New York, NY: Farrar, Straus, and Giroux Publishers.

Questioning the Author Queries Chart

Goal	Queries
Initiate discussion	■ What is the author trying to say? ■ What is the author's message? ■ What is the author talking about?
Help students focus on the author's message	■ That's what the author says, but what does it mean?
Help students link information	■ How does that connect with what the author already told us? ■ How does that fit in with what the author already told us? ■ What information has the author added here that connects to or fits in with _____?
Identify difficulties with the way the author has presented information	■ Does that make sense? ■ Is that said in a clear way? ■ Did the author explain that clearly? . . . Why or why not? . . . What's missing? . . . What do we need to figure out or find out?
Encourage students to refer back to the text either because they have misinterpreted a statement or to help them recognize that they have made an inference	■ Did the author tell us that? ■ Did the author give us the answer to that?
Encourage students to recognize plot development	■ What do you think the author is getting at here? . . . What's going on? . . . What's happening? ■ What has the author told us now?
Motivate students to consider how problems are addressed or solved	■ So, how did the author settle that for us? ■ How did the author work that out for us?
Help students recognize author's technique	■ How has the author let you know that something has changed in the story? ■ How is the author painting a picture here? ■ How did the author let you see something/ feel something/smell something? ■ What has the author told us that (character's name) doesn't know? ■ What is the author doing here? . . . How did the author create humor/ suspense/ sadness, etc? . . . Why do you suppose the author used foreshadowing/ flashback, etc?
Prompt students to consider characters' thoughts and actions	■ How do things look for (character's name) now? ■ What is the author trying to tell us about _____ (character's name)?
Prompt students to predict what a character might do	■ Given what the author has already told us, how do you think (character's name) will handle the situation?

Adapted from: Beck, I. L., McKeown, M. G., Hamilton, R. L., & Kucan, L. (1997). *Questioning the author: An approach for enhancing student engagement with text.* Newark, DE: International Reading Association.

Directed Reading-Thinking Activity (DR-TA)

The DR-TA instructional strategy consists of a **sequence of three questions** that may be asked during content area instruction while engaging in discussion of a text. Developed by Stauffer (1969), this simple questioning procedure helps readers develop strong comprehension and higher level thinking by asking them to combine their prediction strategies with information found in the text to support their assertions. The three questions, in sequence, are:

1. "**What** do you think?" or "What do you think will happen next?"
2. "**Why** do you think so?" or "Why do you think this will happen?"
3. "**Can** you **prove** it?" or "What else might happen?" (An important consideration with this question is to ask the reader to provide evidence or to support his/her answer to #1 and #2 with evidence from the text or from prior learning.)

For **expository texts**, teachers can follow the steps below as they implement the DR-TA strategy:

1. Identify the purpose of the reading. Begin with a quick survey of the title, subheadings, illustrations, etc. Ask predicting question "**What do you think this chapter/section will be about?**" (**#1**) Record predictions on board and ask "**Why do you think so?**" (**#2**) Encourage guided discussion.
2. Adjust the rate and amount of reading (each predetermined chunk to be read silently) to the purposes and nature of the material.
3. Ask students to read silently to that predetermined logical stopping point in the text. Use a 3 × 5 or 5 × 8 index card for students to place on the page so as not to read ahead before answering questions. Observe the reading (of individual students to see amount of difficulty they may have with comprehension, vocabulary, etc.).
4. Guide reader-text interactions. This can be done during discussion time. Students are encouraged to rework predictions as they read and write down revisions.
5. Extend learning through discussion, further reading, additional study, or writing.
   a. after reading, students are asked if predictions were inaccurate, if they had to revise or reject any predictions, how they knew revision was necessary, and what their new predictions were
   b. small group discussion is useful at this time
   c. teacher asks open-ended questions that encourage generalization and application relevant to students' predictions and significant concepts presented
6. Ask proof from students for their predictions, ideas. "**How do you know that?**" "**Why did you think so?**" **What made you think that way?**" (**#3**) Students should share passages, sentences, etc., for further proof.

Adapted from: Stauffer, R. G. (1969). *Directing reading maturity as a cognitive process*. New York, NY: Harper Row.

Question-Answer Relationships (QAR)

Question–Answer Relationships (Raphael, 1984) can be incorporated into a guided reading approach to comprehension. It is an instructional approach for alerting students to differences in types of questions and in the answers required. It consists of **two broad categories** of questions: *in-the-book* and *in-my head* (Raphael, 1986). These refer to the source of information needed in constructing both a question and an answer. See below:

In-the-book questions and answers—deal with information that is explicitly in the text

In-my head questions and answers—focus on prior knowledge and/or textual information

Both of these two broad categories of questions and answers are divided into other kinds of questions. See below:

In-the-book questions and answers are further divided into *right-there* and *think-and-search* questions and answers. See below:

Right-there questions and answers—the words used to make up the question and the words used to answer the question are found in the same text sentence. **"Oh, the answer is right here. It says . . ."**

Think-and-search questions and answers—words for the question and words for the answer are not found in a single sentence. Rather, readers must pull together different parts of the reading to answer the question. In other words, the reader will find the answer in more than one place in the text. **"Hmmm, based on what it said on page 26, and what it says here, the answer is . . . ."**

In-my-head questions and answers are also further divided into **author-and-you** and **on-my-own** questions and answers. See below:

Author-and-you questions and answers—an answer comes from what students know, what is in the text, and how the two kinds of information fit together. **"Based on what the book says in chapter 5, and what I already know about . . ., the answer is . . . ."**

On-my-own questions and answers—students use only their own knowledge and experience. These questions can be answered without reading a text. **"Well, we've learned about . . . last year, and I experienced this myself, so I know the answer is . . . ."**

The teacher can conduct a discussion about the information in the text using questions modeled from the QAR format. Or, the teacher can create a question sheet in which all questions are labeled by the category of QAR question in order to help the reader know where the question originates, thus knowing where the answer is found.

Raphael, T. E. (1984). Teaching learners about sources of information for answering comprehension questions. *Journal of Reading, 27,* 303–311.

Raphael, T. E. (1986). Teaching Question Answer Relationships, revisited. *The Reading Teacher, 39*(6), 516–522.

Text Structures

When teachers help students to identify text patterns in expository texts through explicit instruction, they are equipping them with powerful strategies for effective reading and learning in the content areas. After students become familiar with these patterns, teachers may enhance their learning by presenting specific graphic organizers (as shown on the following pages) that correlate with the text patterns in this chart. Students learn that these graphic organizers become useful tools for gleaning key information from texts.

Description/List	providing information about a topic, concept, event, object, person, idea, and so on, usually qualifying the listing by criteria such as size or importance
	This pattern connects ideas through description by listing the important characteristics or attributes of the topic under consideration. This is the most common textbook organization.
	■ Signal Words . . . such as, for example, like
Sequence	putting facts, events, or concepts into a sequence
	The author traces the development of the topic or gives the steps in the process. Time reference may be explicit or implicit, but a sequence is evident. May be chronological order, process order (steps to do or make something), order by size (largest to smallest, vice versa), order by place (location), or order of importance (most to least importance or vice versa).
	■ Signal Words . . . first, next, second, last, before, afterwards, another, finally
Compare-contrast	Explains how two or more people, places, phenomena, ideas, concepts are alike or different
	■ comparison—pointing out the likenesses among facts, people, events, concepts, etc.
	■ contrast—pointing out the differences between facts, people, events, concepts, etc.
	■ Signal Words . . . same/different, like/unlike, although, yet, while, however
Cause-effect	showing how facts, events, or concepts (effects) happen or come into being because of other facts, events, or concepts (causes)
	Shows causal relationships between phenomena; something takes place that causes something else to happen, or something is "in place" that results in something happening, such as "It rained so hard for so long that it caused the rivers to flood their banks." (example of something taking place that causes something else to happen); "The moon's gravitational force on the earth causes high tides and low tides." (example of something that's already "in place" that results in something happening).
	■ Signal Words . . . since, because, as a result, if . . . then
Problem-Solution	showing the development of a problem and these solution(s) to the problem
	■ may include the solution(s) to the problem
	■ sometimes includes the process needed to come to a conclusion
	■ implies that the reader may develop a step by step process that leads to a solution
	■ Signal Words . . . question, answer, thus, accordingly, decide
Classification	different details relating to a topic are arranged in categories, or groups
	It identifies categories, shows how various examples in the same category are alike, and shows how the separate categories are different. This text pattern may also show how a large subject may be broken up into different parts.
	■ Signal Words . . . there are, for example, as well as, some, other, just as

Adapted from: Vacca, R. T., & Vacca, J. L. (1996). *Content area reading*. (2nd ed.). New York, NY: Little Brown.
Adapted from: Wiener, H. S., & Bazerman, C. (1994). *Reading skills handbook*. (6th ed.). Boston, MA: Houghton Mifflin.

Graphic Organizers for Text Patterns

Problem-Solution Chart	

What is the problem?	

Whose problem is it? Why is it a problem?	

What are three possible solutions? 1.	Pros and Cons for each solution (+) (--)
2.	(+) (--)
3.	(+) (--)

What is the best solution and why?	

Guiding Questions for Analysis for Problem-Solution:
What is the problem that is presented?
Who owns the problem?
Why is it a problem?
What are three possible solutions to the problem?
What are some benefits and disadvantages of each
   possible solution?
Which solution offers the best possible outcome?
Explain why.

Cause-Effect (Fishbone)

Guiding Questions for Analysis for Fishbone Map:
What are the factors that caused the scenario (event,
   experiment, etc?)
How are they interrelated?

Compare/Contrast Chart (Matrix)

	Feature 1	Feature 2	Feature 3
Name 1			
Name 2			
Name 3			

Guiding Questions for Analysis for Compare/Contrast/ Matrix:
What is being compared?
What are the similarities?
What are the differences?
What features do they have in common?

Sequence (Cycle)	Sequence (Chain of Events)

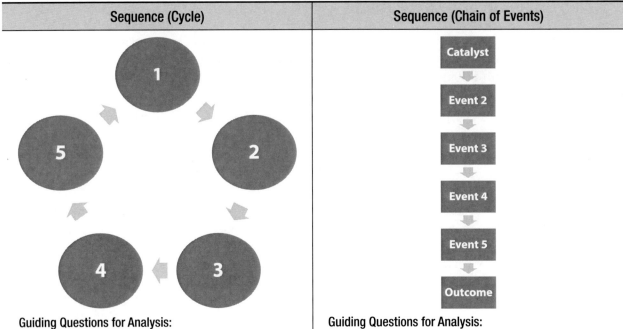

Guiding Questions for Analysis:
What are the key events in the cycle?
How are these events related?
In what ways do they keep the process going?

Guiding Questions for Analysis:
What is the initiating event or catalyst?
What stages or steps follow that event or catalyst?
How does one lead to another in a progression?
What is the final outcome?

Description/List (Semantic Web)	Classification (Hierarchy Web)

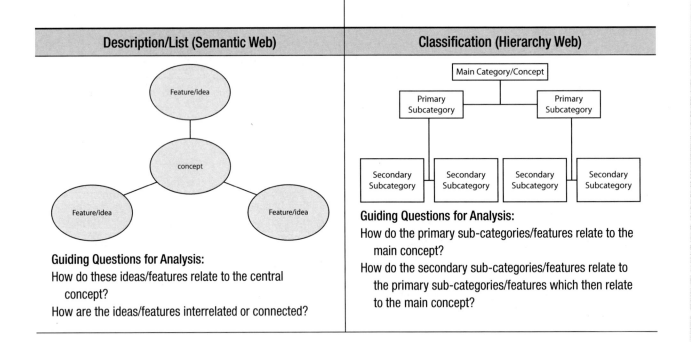

Guiding Questions for Analysis:
How do these ideas/features relate to the central
  concept?
How are the ideas/features interrelated or connected?

Guiding Questions for Analysis:
How do the primary sub-categories/features relate to the
  main concept?
How do the secondary sub-categories/features relate to
  the primary sub-categories/features which then relate
  to the main concept?

Adapted by: Alice F. Snyder, 2000, from course materials, I&L 2212, Methods and Materials in Teaching Reading (1995), University of Pittsburgh, Pittsburgh, PA.

Critical Reading and Viewing: Types of Propaganda Techniques

One aspect of critical reading that readers must understand and learn to recognize is **propaganda.** Propaganda is a systematic dissemination or promotion of particular ideas, doctrines, or practices to further one's own cause or to damage an opposing one through the use of words and nonverbal symbols. In short, it is an "attempt to persuade others to accept certain beliefs or opinions" (Gunning, 2000, p. 284). Elementary students not only encounter propaganda techniques in written texts, but they also encounter propaganda every day through television and electronic media. When readers learn, through careful, thoughtful instruction, that the purpose of propaganda is to sway their judgment and opinion, they become critical readers who are better equipped to make informed judgments based on the facts rather than basing their judgments on emotional appeals of propaganda. There are several types of propaganda techniques, and the following are most frequently taught in schools.

1. **Testimonial**
   "Well-known personalities testify or speak out for an idea or product. This technique is frequently used in advertisements in which a sports star endorses a shampoo or a TV star urges consumers to buy a certain brand of toothpaste." [Most widely used, easiest to understand—Start with testimonial]
2. **Bandwagon**
   "Playing on the natural desire to be part of the crowd, this technique tries to convince by stating that because so many others are buying a product or taking certain action, we should too."
3. **Card stacking**
   "This method lists all the good points or advantages of an idea or product but none of its bad points or disadvantages."
4. **Plain Folks**
   "To win our trust, a person of power or wealth tries to convince us that she or he is an ordinary person just like us."
5. **Name calling**
   "Words that may have unfavorable connotations such as *nerd, tightwad, liberal,* or *spendthrift* are used to describe opposing political candidates, competing products, or rival ideas." We respond emotionally to the name, thus failing to consider the people, products, or ideas in a rational manner.
6. **Glittering generalities**
   "The near opposite of name calling, glittering generalities are favorable-sounding abstract terms or scientific words that usually evoke a positive response. Examples are *justice, honesty, new, miracle ingredients,* and scientific-sounding names like *benzoyl peroxide.*"
7. **Transfer**
   "In this device, the favorable feeling we have for a symbol, person, or object is carried over or transferred to an idea or product someone is trying to sell." Example: "A candidate for political office is seen standing next to a flag with her family, which includes a big, friendly collie." The positive feelings we have are transferred to the candidate. (pgs. 284–285)

From: Gunning, T. G. (2000). *Creating literacy for all children.* (3rd ed.). Boston, MA: Allyn and Bacon.

Strategic Reading and Study Guides in the Content Areas

Chapter Three presents a variety of strategic reading and study guides that teachers may use to facilitate the reading process as students construct meaning in all content areas. These guides help students to interact with informational texts in an active, strategic manner which leads to more productive learning from texts. Literacy researchers such as Karen Wood, Diane Lapp, James Flood, and D. Bruce Taylor (2008) have greatly influenced instruction and student interaction with expository texts. Reading and study guides strategically break down texts into manageable chunks or components so that students can become critical readers. As a result, readers pull information from texts and analyze them more effectively. These reading guides then become study tools that increase metacognition. As these tools impact the thinking process, students become independent readers. They become independent readers through the process of adjusting reading rates and analyzing chunks of texts in specific ways. Since students are directed through specific analysis of pages and paragraphs of the text, they learn to read and think through the text with intentionality of purpose.

Strategic Reading Guides

Strategic reading guides engage students as they actively navigate through the reading process. Karen Wood and her colleagues, Diane Lapp, James Flood, and D. Bruce Taylor (2008) promote the use of strategy guides, which are "teacher-developed graphic and questioning guides used to help students organize information as a means to comprehend what they are reading" (p. 4). These guides are catalysts that progressively direct students through the thinking process so they become strategic, independent readers who construct maximum meaning from minimal chunks of text. As students work through the questions and activities in the guide, "they are able to arrange information into categories in a visual and succinct manner that supports their learning and studying" (p. 4). In addition, strategy guides are means for socially constructed knowledge that promote the use of multiple literacies. With the renewed focus placed on reading informational texts by National and State Common Core Standards, it is essential that teachers utilize strategic reading guides to facilitate students' comprehension of content area texts.

When designing a strategic reading guide, it is important to use an innovative approach rather than creating a modified worksheet. Each guide needs to include thought-provoking tasks and questions rather than the traditional objective questions, which are often seen on standardized tests. Students need to generate responses rather than simply making choices among the options they are given. This promotes higher-level thinking and activates deeper levels of engagement with texts.

When choosing and creating strategic reading guides, teachers initially examine the nature and importance of the information presented in the text. Are the concepts and terminology in the text new, familiar, or reviewed? Are there important causal relationships that must be understood in order to interpret the text effectively? What text structures are presented in the pages and paragraphs, such as cause/effect, compare/contract, sequence, description/list, problem-solution, and classification? What reading rate is most appropriate for each section of the text? What material could be skimmed or scanned versus what material should be read with more attention to details? Are there specific visual features, such as charts, graphs, diagrams, maps, and photos that provide important information about concepts and content?

Teachers need to consider the nature and importance of information presented and the expectations for processing the cognitive demands of the text. Strategic reading guides divide the text into small, manageable chunks that are less intimidating for children as they process the information while reading. This can be done by focusing on one or two paragraphs at a time. Since elementary-aged children are novices at reading expository texts, teachers must facilitate their students' reading experiences with strategically designed opportunities to glean main ideas and key details. Teachers include key questions or tasks that support students as they process each paragraph, or chunk, of the text before they are required to move on to the next chunk of material. It is important not to leave out any text in a given section, including visual features, such as charts, graphs, maps, and diagrams, because it may result in creating gaps in a child's conceptual understanding of the material in the text. This may hinder the reader's ability to formulate mental images while constructing meaning from the text.

Whether the text is a content area textbook, an informational picture book, a text read from a website page on the computer, or any narrative texts, strategically designed reading guides support students' interaction with texts. Ultimately, reading guides promote self-efficacy as children become strategic, independent readers who experience success as they make meaning from a wide variety of texts.

Chart for Exploring Strategic Reading Guides

Names of Guide	Description	Purpose	Grade Levels
Anticipation Guide (Extended Anticipation Guide)	■ a list of statements that help students to initially determine their prior knowledge on a topic and then verify or negate their responses during and/or after reading the text.	■ activates or builds background knowledge ■ helps students verify conceptual understanding by revisiting initial responses to statements	All grade levels
Pattern Guide	■ an assorted collection of tasks that take various text structures which are scrambled. Students must carefully think about relationships among the given patterns as they restore the text structures into a logical order.	■ supports students' awareness of organizational structures in expository texts ■ helps students connect the dots and determine textual relationships	Grades 1 and up
Point-of-View Guide	■ a list of questions presented in an interview format that requires students to answer from the perspectives of people who witnessed or participated in significant events relating to history, science, fine arts, etc. Students assume the roles of various real or fictional characters which enhances their ability to empathize.	■ promotes retelling and paraphrasing skills ■ develops mental acuity through elaboration of ideas from multiple sources ■ reinforces content learning	Most appropriate for grades 3 and up
Three Level Guide	■ a list of questions, each relating to the three levels of comprehension, literal, interpretive, applied/evaluative, that cover a section or chapter of a narrative or expository text. Questions are labeled according to their level, which provides students with frameworks for their thinking in order to respond to the questions effectively.	■ actively engages the reader in progressing through the levels of comprehension from explicit ideas to higher levels of abstract and critical thinking ■ fosters affective thinking that builds in-depth comprehension and the ability to connect the ideas/concepts with their lived experiences	Most appropriate for grades 2 and up
Guide-O-Rama	■ a list of questions and/or tasks that guide students through a text in accordance with the rate of reading that suits the significance or the difficulty level of specific pages and/or paragraphs in the text.	■ promotes active reading, awareness of appropriate reading rates, and facets of comprehension based on conceptual load and text difficulty	Most effective for grades 1 and up
Reading Road Map	■ a guide which resembles a "road map" and consists of missions (questions and activities), road signs (reading rate indicators), and location signs (headings, page/paragraph numbers).	■ provides a motivational, visual approach that supports readers' comprehension of expository text and awareness of reading rate	Most appropriate for grades 2 and up

Continued.

Names of Guide	Description	Purpose	Grade Levels
Textbook Activity Guide	■ a research-based guide focusing on self-monitoring strategies and metacognition. The teacher prepares specific tasks for small chunks of the text to help support the reading of more complex information. Tasks vary from explicit question and answer strategies to implicit/ creative activities, such as diagramming and drawing pictures to represent conceptual understanding of the text. Coding systems indicate self-monitoring strategies and activities for completion by individuals or partners.	■ guides exploration of more complex texts by providing a coding system to support reading in smaller chunks ■ promotes the development of active reading strategies for individuals and partners ■ supports student exploration of the structure of a text by serving as an outline that draws attention to headings, subheadings, boldfaced words, and all visual and graphic features of the text	Most appropriate for grades 2 and up
Interactive Guide	■ a management guide in which the teacher pre-assigns students into individual, partner, small group, and whole class reading. The teacher serves as both monitor and guide as he/she conducts the interactions with students using both traditional and non-traditional texts. Over several days of instruction, students develop an understanding of the text as they complete the guide. The teacher serves as a co-constructor of meaning with direct involvement in guiding students as they process the text.	■ provides a visual representation of the teacher's management plan for the text ■ encourages teachers to thoughtfully group students for utilizing strategies and approaches for co-construction of meaning for a given section of the text ■ promotes active engagement for exploring the text through peer tutoring, small groups, and whole-class instruction	All grade levels
Analogical Guide	■ a guide that takes abstract concepts and associates them with familiar, everyday concepts through pictures and words ■ Teachers identify the concepts, create and illustrate appropriate analogies, and explain them.	■ provides a connection between the new and the known ■ promotes deeper understanding of vocabulary concepts by comparing terminology	Most appropriate for grades 2 and up

Extended Anticipation Guide (Intermediate Grades)

Directions: Before reading the book *Snowflake Bentley,* read each statement with your partner. Decide if you **agree** or **disagree** with the statement. Circle the **thumbs-up if you agree** or the **thumbs-down if you disagree** with the statement. Then, read "Snowflake Bentley" with your partner. After reading, decide if you still agree or disagree with each statement and circle the thumbs-up or thumbs-down for each statement under the AFTER column. Write a brief statement justifying your response.

Snowflake Bentley

By Jacqueline Briggs Martin

Before	Statement	After	Justify
	1. Snow is a form of moisture.		
	2. All snowflakes have six branches, or points.		
	3. Snowflakes are made up of ice crystals and air.		
	4. All snowflakes look alike and have the same design.		
	5. It is impossible to take a picture of a snowflake because it melts too quickly.		

Extended Anticipation Guide

Amos and Boris, by William Steig

A. Read each statement and circle **Agree** if you agree with the statement and **Disagree** if you do not agree with the statement.

Explanation with Story Evidence

1. Whales and mice are very different kinds of animals.

   Agree   Disagree

   _____

   _____

   _____

2. Mice do not like the water.

   Agree   Disagree

   _____

   _____

   _____

3. Whales are dangerous, mean creatures.

   Agree   Disagree

   _____

   _____

   _____

4. Whales are fish.

   Agree   Disagree

   _____

   _____

   _____

5. Mice are mammals.

   Agree   Disagree

   _____

   _____

   _____

6. Whales can live away from water.

   Agree   Disagree

   _____

   _____

   _____

B. After reading the book, *Amos and Boris* (1971), go back and think about your answers above. You may change your answers if you think it is necessary. If you do, explain why you changed your response on the lines above. Include evidence from the story in your explanation. You may also want to read the book *Whales* (1993) or other informational texts in print form or from the Internet.

Steig, W. (1971). *Amos and Boris.* New York, NY: Farrar, Straus, and Giroux.

Jeunesse, G., Delafosse, C., Fuhr, U., & Sautai, R. (1993). *Whales.* New York, NY: Scholastic.

Sequential Pattern Guide

Sequence Chain of Events Guide

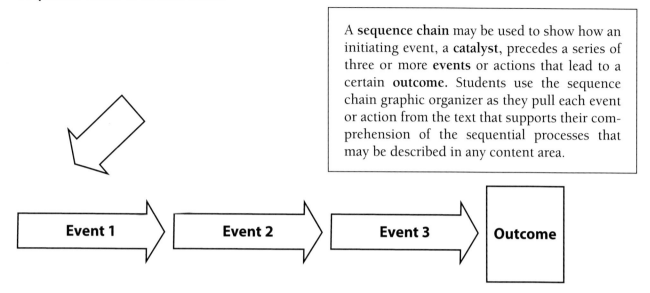

A **sequence chain** may be used to show how an initiating event, a **catalyst**, precedes a series of three or more **events** or actions that lead to a certain **outcome**. Students use the sequence chain graphic organizer as they pull each event or action from the text that supports their comprehension of the sequential processes that may be described in any content area.

Sequence Cycle Guide

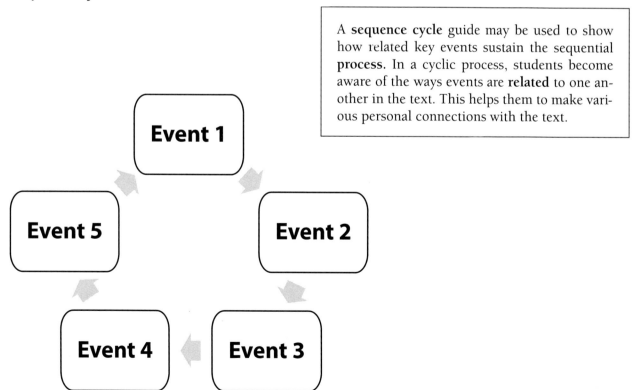

A **sequence cycle** guide may be used to show how related key events sustain the sequential **process**. In a cyclic process, students become aware of the ways events are **related** to one another in the text. This helps them to make various personal connections with the text.

Cause/Effect Pattern Guide-Fourth Grade

Revolutionary War

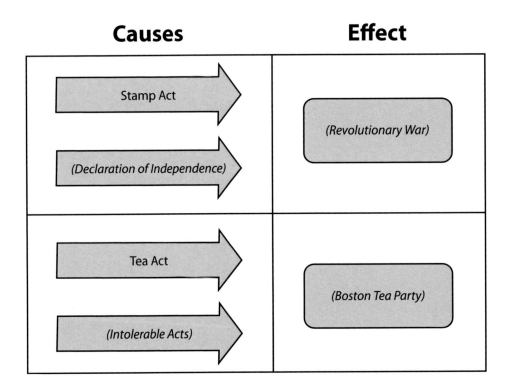

Causes   **Effect**

Stamp Act

(Declaration of Independence)

(Revolutionary War)

Tea Act

(Intolerable Acts)

(Boston Tea Party)

Directions: Use the clue in each **cause** arrow to think about what **effect** occurred as a result. Choose an **effect** from the *List of Effects* below and write it in the box under **Effect**. Then determine and find a second **cause** from the *List of Causes* below that also led to the **effect** (event) and write it in the second arrow under **Causes**.

List of Causes
Intolerable Acts
Stamp Act
Tea Act
Declaration of Independence
British Troops Marching to Lexington and Concord

List of Effects
Boston Tea Party
Revolutionary War
Paul Revere's Ride

Problem-Solution Pattern Guide

What is/was the problem?

Whose problem is/was it? Why is/was it a problem?

Possible solutions?	Pros and Cons for each solution
1.	(+)
	(--)
2.	(+)
	(--)
3.	(+)
	(--)

What may be the best solution and why?

Adapted by: Alice F. Snyder, 2000, from course materials, I&L 2212 (1995), *Methods and Materials in Teaching Reading,* University of Pittsburgh, Pittsburgh, PA.

Compare-Contrast Pattern Guide

Major Topic/Idea/Event	What is being compared or contrasted?	Major Topic/Idea/Event

Example:

Woodland Tribes	Cultural Aspects	Plains Tribes
Birchbark canoes On foot Dugout canoes	Methods of transportation	Horse On foot
Small game (squirrels, fox, etc.), deer Fish Berries, corn, beans, squash	What they ate	Meat from buffalo Deer, small animals found on the plains/prairies berries
Animal skin Leggings Loin cloths	Their clothing	Buffalo skin leggings, tunics, loin cloths Headdresses with eagle feathers depending on status
Wigwams made from bark of trees and thatch	Their houses	Tepees made of buffalo hides and poles from tree branches
	Geography of the region where they lived	
	Their customs	
	Status of women in tribe	

Adapted from: Norton, T., & Jackson Land, B. L. (2008). *50 literacy strategies for beginning teachers, 1–8.* (2nd ed.). Upper Saddle River, NJ: Merrill/Prentice Hall. (pp. 112)

Point-of-View Guide

Brittni Chafin
Kennesaw State University
Chapter 8 Lesson 2: Immigrants in America—Grade 5

You are about to be interviewed as if you were a person living in the United States in the late nineteenth century. Consult your text book in order to accurately describe your reaction to the events discussed below. *Note: **Answers are in italics after each question.**

Arriving in America (pg. 266)

As a Jewish immigrant:

1. What was your reason for moving to the United States? (paragraph 2)

   I moved to the U.S. to prevent being hurt or killed because of my religion.

2. What were reasons other than your own that caused people to migrate to the United States? (paragraph 2)

   They wanted to find work, political freedom, and to escape from war.

Immigration Stations (p. 267)

3. You are a European immigrant who went through the immigration station in New York. Tell me the name of that station and describe your experience. (paragraph 1)

   I went through the immigration station, Ellis Island. After reaching the port, I was asked where I planned to live and work. When I told the government officials that I did not know, they yelled at me. Then doctors examined me to make sure that I did not have any diseases. After they made sure I was healthy, they allowed me to leave Ellis Island and enter America.

4. As an immigrant who moved to the United States from Asia, what immigration station did you go through? Tell me about your experience coming through this immigration station as an Asian immigrant in the mid to late 1800s. (paragraph 2)

   I went through the immigration station, Angel Island in San Francisco Bay. From what I heard, we faced more prejudice than immigrants who went through Ellis Island. I had to stay at Angel Island for three months before I was allowed to enter the United States, and some people were even sent home.

Living in a New Country (p. 268)

As a recent immigrant to the United States:

5. Now that you are a new immigrant who has been permitted to enter the U.S., how will you choose where you will live? (paragraph 1)

   I decided to move into the neighborhood where my family and friends already live.

6. Do you have anything in common with the people who live around you, and if so, please describe some of those things. (paragraph 1)

   My neighborhood only had people who were in my ethnic group. We all speak the same language, practice the same religion, and have the same customs.

7. Now that you have lived in the U.S. for a couple of months, do you like it? Has it been easier or harder than you expected? Explain why. (paragraph 2)

   Although the United States is better than the country I am from, life is still hard. I was not expecting life to be this difficult. I did not know that I was going to have to work in a dirty factory to support my family. I thought that I would be paid more and live in a nicer house.

8. Although you were fortunate enough to get a nice apartment, your friend Claude had to live in a tenement. Would you describe the conditions of his tenement and explain why he wanted to move so badly? (paragraph 3)

   Claude's tenement is very unsafe because it was poorly built, and it is overcrowded. Another reason that he hates living there is because the tenement has no windows or running water.

Hard Times for Immigrants (p. 268)

9. As an immigrant trying to get a job in a steel factory, why do you have an advantage over someone who was not an immigrant? (paragraph 4)

   I have an advantage because most factory owners like hiring immigrants because we work hard and do not ask for a high wage.

10. As an American who lived in the United States your entire life, why do you want immigration to stop? (paragraph 4)

    I want immigration to stop because I am scared that they will take my job.

Laws against Immigration (p. 269)

11. You are a person living in Asia during the year 1883. Why is your dream of moving to America probably not going to happen? (paragraph 1)

    I will probably not be able to move to the United States because they just passed a law, the Chinese Exclusion Act, and it was created to keep out new Chinese immigrants.

12. As an immigrant living in the United States during the year 1925, how were you treated? (paragraph 2)

    I have been treated very poorly, and I often face prejudice.

13. After many challenging years of living in the United States, you and a large group of immigrants receive recognition for your contributions to this country. What are some examples of your contributions that helped the U.S. become one of the richest and fastest-growing countries in the world? (paragraph 2)

    I helped to build railroad tracks which expanded railroad transportation across the country. Other immigrants are being recognized for their work digging deep coal mines and in factories.

Three Level Guide

Intermediate Level-Science Lesson on Adaptations

Instructions: Read pages 42–51 in your science book, "What are some ways mammals are adaptable?" and answer the following questions with a partner.

A. **Literal Level** (answers found in the book)
   1. What is an animal's environment? (pg. 42, paragraph 1)
   2. Provide examples of how the mule deer adapt to their environment. (pg. 42, paragraph 2)
   3. Why do the nightjar bird's feathers look like the forest floor? (pg. 44, paragraph 2)
   4. Why are the penguin's feathers waterproof? (pg. 45, paragraph 1)
   5. _____ are a body part on fish that help them get oxygen from water. (pg. 46, paragraph 1)
   6. What adaptation do catfish have that helps them find food? (pg. 47, paragraph 1)
   7. Give examples of how the desert iguana makes adaptations to live in its environment. (pg. 49, paragraph 1)

B. **Inferential Level** (Think about what you read and search for the answer; it may be found as the main idea of a paragraph, or it may be why something was caused.)
   1. How does camouflage help an animal stay safe from other animals that may want to hunt or harm it?
   2. Hummingbirds and penguins are alike and different. Name a few similarities or differences.
   3. Why do catfish need feelers to help them find food?
   4. Why does a snake's mouth open wide to swallow food whole?

C. **Generalization/Evaluative Level** (Questions will be answered on your own by thinking and applying what you know about the topic.)
   1. Why and in what ways do you think the chipmunk plans ahead for winter?
   2. People adapt to their environment. Offer a few examples from your life experiences.
   3. What color do you predict most desert animals are? Why do you predict that color?

Review: Think back to our class discussion on classifying questions. Below the follow questions, write the level (Literal, Inferential, or Generalization/Evaluative) each belongs to. After identifying each, turn to your partner and create at least one question for each level using the text you just read. These questions will be shared and charted with the class.

Part 1
1. What is camouflage?
   Type of Question: _____
2. Why does a rapid change in weather affect how quickly a snake moves?
   Type of Question: _____
3. In your opinion, why is it important for animals to adapt?
   Type of Question: _____

Part 2
Literal Level Question: _____

_____

Inferential Level Question: _____

_____

Generalization/Evaluative Level Question: _____

_____

Guide-O-Rama—Grade 5

Lesson 5: What are Food Chains and Webs?
Pages 202–213

Pages 202–203, Title and Focus Questions
Skim the title and focus questions. Keep these questions in mind as you read the lesson.

Page 204, Paragraphs 1 and 2
Paragraph 1 introduces two key terms, **food chain** and **food web**. Be sure to read this carefully and be able to define these terms. Read paragraph 2 and describe an **ecosystem.**

Page 204, the Diagram
First, follow the arrows on the diagram and describe the ways the diagram illustrates the food chain. Refer to paragraph 1 for evidence.

Page 205, Paragraph 1
Read to determine the value of nutrients in plants and animals. Why are nutrients important? Think of ten ways you use energy every day.

Page 205, Paragraph 2
Skim to refresh your memory about the importance of sunlight and the ways energy is passed along the food chain. Describe a sequence of energy exchange.

Page 205, Paragraph 3
Read carefully to be able to explain how **herbivores** and **carnivores absorb** energy as part of the food web.

Page 206, Paragraph 1
Paragraph 1 introduces the Energy Pyramid diagram at the bottom of the page. Read it quickly.

Page 206, Energy Pyramid
Scan the Energy Pyramid diagram to be able to explain how it aligns with ideas from paragraph 1.

Page 206, Paragraphs 2 and 3
Identify the primary producers in a food chain or web. How do the primary producers make their food?

Bereiter, C., Biemiller, A., Campione, J., Carruthers, I., Fuchs, D., Fuchs, L., et al. (2008). *SRA Imagine it!* Columbus, OH: McGraw Hill.
Wood, K. D., Lapp, D., & Flood, J. (1992). *Guiding readers through text: A review of study guides.* Newark, DE: International Reading Association.
Dove, rabbit, and turtle images © Shutterstock, Inc.

Reading Road Map—Fourth Grade

Christopher Brown
Kennesaw State University
Conquest of the Americas (pg. 104–107)

Overall Mission: You are about to learn about how the Americas were discovered and explored.

Location	Speed	Mission

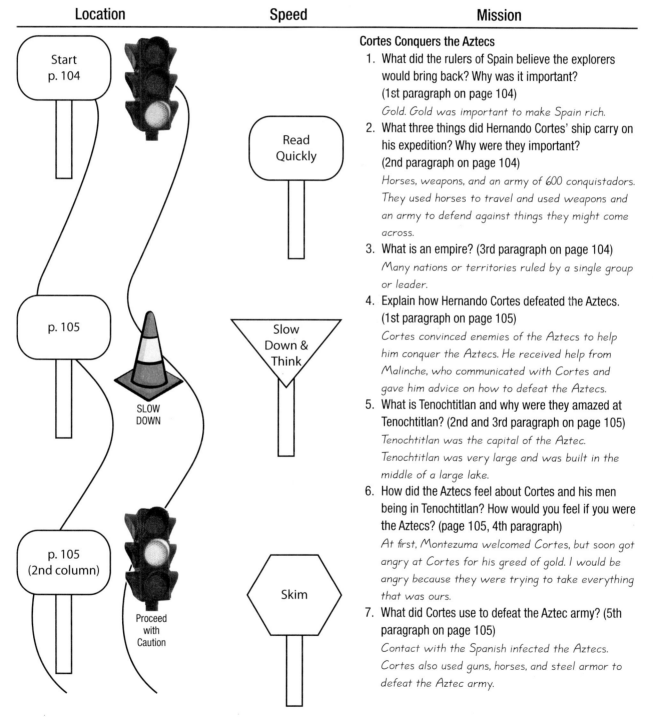

Cortes Conquers the Aztecs

1. What did the rulers of Spain believe the explorers would bring back? Why was it important? (1st paragraph on page 104)

   Gold. Gold was important to make Spain rich.

2. What three things did Hernando Cortes' ship carry on his expedition? Why were they important? (2nd paragraph on page 104)

   Horses, weapons, and an army of 600 conquistadors. They used horses to travel and used weapons and an army to defend against things they might come across.

3. What is an empire? (3rd paragraph on page 104)

   Many nations or territories ruled by a single group or leader.

4. Explain how Hernando Cortes defeated the Aztecs. (1st paragraph on page 105)

   Cortes convinced enemies of the Aztecs to help him conquer the Aztecs. He received help from Malinche, who communicated with Cortes and gave him advice on how to defeat the Aztecs.

5. What is Tenochtitlan and why were they amazed at Tenochtitlan? (2nd and 3rd paragraph on page 105)

   Tenochtitlan was the capital of the Aztec. Tenochtitlan was very large and was built in the middle of a large lake.

6. How did the Aztecs feel about Cortes and his men being in Tenochtitlan? How would you feel if you were the Aztecs? (page 105, 4th paragraph)

   At first, Montezuma welcomed Cortes, but soon got angry at Cortes for his greed of gold. I would be angry because they were trying to take everything that was ours.

7. What did Cortes use to defeat the Aztec army? (5th paragraph on page 105)

   Contact with the Spanish infected the Aztecs. Cortes also used guns, horses, and steel armor to defeat the Aztec army.

Green light, slow cone, and yellow light © Shutterstock, Inc.

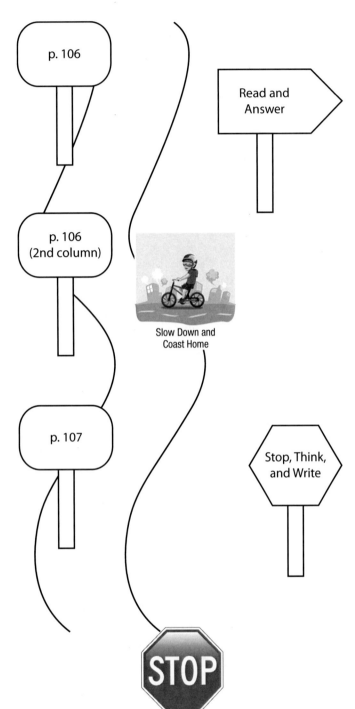

p. 106

p. 106
(2nd column)

p. 107

Read and
Answer

Slow Down and
Coast Home

Stop, Think,
and Write

STOP

Exploring North America

8. Who was the first person to reach land that is now the United States? What was he looking for? Did he find it? (1st paragraph on page 106)

   Juan Ponce de Leon was looking for gold and the Fountain of Youth. No, it was just a legend, and it was not true.

9. Identify two accomplishments of Hernando De Soto. (2nd, 3rd, and 4th paragraphs on page 106)

   De Soto settled lands beyond Florida, and he reached the Mississippi River.

10. Why was Francisco Vasquez de Coronado exploring North America? (5th paragraph on page 106)

   Coronado was looking for cities of gold that he heard about in legends.

Cities of Gold

11. Who were the first Europeans to see the Grand Canyon? (page 107)

   Coronado's soldiers were the first.

12. Where is the Grand Canyon located? (page 107)

   It is in Arizona.

13. Why were European explorers searching North American cities? (1st paragraph on page 107)

   They were looking for cities of gold.

14. Recall three obstacles conquistadors faced. (2nd paragraph on page 107)

   They traveled long distances, encountered bad weather, and suffered from starvation.

15. Choose an explorer and tell things that you liked and disliked about him.

   Hernando de Soto. I like how he explored the region that we live in. I found it interesting that he found the Mississippi River. I do not like how he enslaved American Indians whom he encountered.

16. If you had the opportunity, would you have been part of the explorer's crew? Explain.

   I would have been a part of the crew. It seems exciting and there would be a chance for me to get rich and famous.

Viola, H. (2005). *Social studies. United States history: Early years.* Boston, MA: Houghton Mifflin.
Kid on bike and STOP sign © Shutterstock, Inc.

Textbook Activity Guide (TAG)-Grade 3

Steven Acquafresca
Kennesaw State University
Chapter 2 Lesson 3 What Are Some Types of Soil? (pages 80–91)

Strategy Codes:
RR-   Read and retell in your own words
DP-   Read and discuss with your partner
PP-   Predict with a partner
WR-   Write a response on your own
Skim-   Read quickly for purpose stated and discuss with partner
MOC-   Organize information with a map, chart, or outline

Self-Monitoring Codes:

___✔___   I understand this information.

___?___   I'm not sure if I understand.

___✗___   I do not understand and I need to restudy.

1. ___✔___ PP-   Pages 80–89. Survey the title of this section, the pictures, charts, and headings. What do you expect to learn in this lesson?

    Possible prediction/discussion: This lesson is going to be about soil. We will probably learn about the different layers of soil and the different kinds of soil. We will also most likely discuss how soil is formed, items that make-up soil, and what soil is used for on a daily basis.

2. ___✔___ PP-   This lesson is going to be about characteristics of soil. Before reading, predict what you think makes up soil, what soil is used for, how old soil is, and/or if soil ever changes.

    Possible prediction: I think soil is made up of small pieces of dirt. People use soil when planting flowers, trees, and different types of foods. Some animals use soil as food. Soil helps grass grow and keeps landforms and trees from eroding away. I think soil is very old and has been on Earth since the beginning of time. Since it is so old, I do not think it changes.

3. ___✔___ WR-   Page 80. Read the "Georgia Fast Fact" at the bottom of the page. How long does it take to form soil?

    It takes between 3,000 and 12,000 years for soil to form.

4. ___✔___ DP-   Page 80. Discuss some crops that grow well in Georgia. Where/When have you seen these crops before?

    Possible discussion: Peanuts, pecans, cotton, peaches, apples, and Vidalia onions grow well in Georgia. I have seen peanuts, pecans, and onion fields when I drove through South Georgia with my family on vacation. There is lots of farm land where these crops grow on I–75 in South Georgia. I have also seen peach and apple trees in the North Georgia Mountains where it is cooler and snows more in the winter.

5. ___✔___ Skim-   Page 81. These vocabulary terms come up throughout the section. DISCUSS the pronunciation of the terms with your partner.

    (Students will look at the words, definitions, and pronunciation guide and will try to sound out each word.)

Pages 82 & 83 give directions for a "guided inquiry" we will do in class another day.

6. ___✔___ RR-   Read page 84, first paragraph under "Layers of Soil." Why is soil important?

Soil helps plants grow and provides places for many animals to live.

7. ___✔___ WR-   Read page 84, 2nd paragraph under "Layers of Soil." What is soil made up of? What is **humus?**

Soil is made up of water, air, humus, dead plants and animals, and tiny pieces of rock. Humus is a section of soil that is made up of parts of dead plants and animals.

8. ___✔___ MOC-   Page 84. Make a brief sequence graphic organizer that shows how humus forms in the soil.

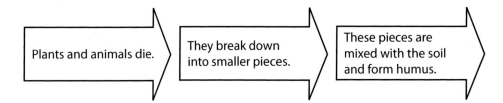

9. ___✔___ WR-   After reading the 2nd paragraph under "Layers of Soil" on page 84, describe 3 to 4 steps pine needles would go through as they become humus.

First, the pine needles would fall from the tree they grew on. Next, they would hit the ground and over time, they would break down into smaller parts. After this, they would become humus (the part of the soil that is made up of parts of dead plants and animals).

10. ___?___ DP-   Read page 85, top paragraph. Explain how soil close to the Earth's surface is different from soil that is deeper down. Where would you find most animals that live in soil?

Possible explanation/discussion: The soil closer to the Earth's surface has more humus and fewer rocks than the soil deeper down. Most animals that live in soil are found just below the surface, rather than deep underground.

11. ___✔___ MOC-   Read the diagram on page 85. Label the diagram showing the 3 different layers of soil. Describe at least one characteristic of each type.

Which layer of soil contains the most humus? Topsoil contains the most humus compared to the other layers of soil.

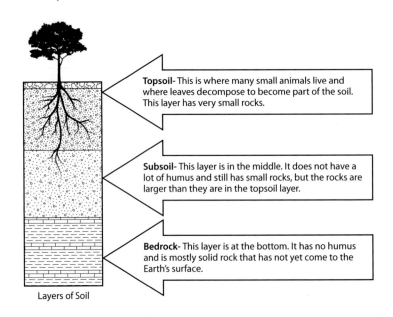

Layers of Soil

12. ___✔___ RR-   Read page 86, 1st paragraph under "Different types of Soil." Retell ways soils can be different from each other.

Possible discussion: Soils can have different colors, different amounts of water, different amounts of humus, and different particle (rock) sizes.

13. ___✔___ PP-   Look at the pictures on pages 86 and 87. Predict characteristics scientists may use to compare different types of soils.

Possible prediction/discussion: Scientists may compare the different colors of the soil and where the soil was originally located when looking for different types.

14. ___✔___ WR-   Read page 86, 2nd paragraph under "Different Types of Soil" and p.87 1st sentence of 1st paragraph. What is **sand**? Have you ever been to the beach? Discuss how sand felt on your feet and what happened when you tried to build a sand castle.

Sand is soil that has small pieces of rock that is visible to the eye. The last time I went to the beach, the sand felt soft and smooth when I walked on it. It felt like my feet sank right into the Earth. It is easy to pick up a pile of sand and see one grain (or one small rock) in it. When sand gets wet, you can easily see footprints. It is hard to build a sand castle with dry sand. As the castle starts to get high, it falls over. I think it is best to build a sand castle with sand that is moist. Sometimes we used to bring water from the Gulf over to the sand so that it was easier to work with, but the water quickly sucked into the sand and in a few minutes, the sand was dry again.

15. ___✔___ WR-   Read page 87, 1st paragraph. In your own words, describe the difference between **sand**, **silt**, and **clay**.

Sand is made up of small grains of rock that can be seen with the eye. Silt soils have tiny grains of rock that are too small to see without a microscope. Clay soils have very, very tiny grains of rock that cannot be felt when you touch the soil.

16. ___✔___ DP-   Look at the pictures on pages 86 and 87 again. Read their captions. Explain the differences between the types of soil shown. Revise your predictions about what scientists look for when classifying soils.

Possible Discussion: The soil on page 86 is mostly sand. The small grains of rock in sand are large enough to be seen without a microscope or magnifying glass. The soil on page 87 looks like clay. This soil has grains of rock that are so small that you cannot feel or see them without a microscope. The sandy soil also looks lighter than the clay soil on page 87. After reading, I think scientists look at the different sizes of rocks and particles in the sand, as well as its color, when classifying soils as sand, silt, or clay.

17. ___✔___ MOC-   Read page 87, 2nd paragraph. Make a chart comparing sand, silt, and clay soils.

Soil Type	Sand	Silt	Clay
Particle Size	Small, but the largest compared to the other types of soil.	Small. Can only be seen with a microscope or hand lens.	Extremely tiny. Can only be seen with a microscope. Can't even feel the particles.

18. ___✔___ DP-   Read page 88, 1st paragraph under "Water and Soils." Describe a time you were using soil when it was wet. How did the wet soil feel? How is this different from dry soil?

Possible discussion: Last spring I was planting a garden and the soil was wet and muddy. It felt sticky and slimy. When soil is dry, it feels like sand and comes off my hands and clothes easily. When it is wet, it is harder to get off my hands and clothes unless I wash them.

19. ___✔___ WR-   Read page 88, 2nd paragraph under "Water and Soils." Explain what makes the reddish color in some soils.

Soils that drain water quickly provide more room for air to get into the soil. The extra air combines with iron, which leads to a bright reddish color in the soil.

20. ✔ RR-   Read page 88, 3rd paragraph under "Water and Soils." Retell what you learned in this paragraph to your partner.

Possible response: Soils that hold more water are usually darker and contain more humus.

21. ✔ WR-   Look at the pictures on page 88. Read their captions. Using the information you just read on this page, infer why wet soils are a darker color than dry soils.

Wet soils are a darker color than dry soils because wet soils contain more humus (dead plants and small animals) which adds a darker color to the soil. Also, the added water takes the place of air which is able to get into dry soils and combine with iron to make the soil appear a lighter color.

22. ✔ MOC-   After reading page 88, make a chart showing the differences between wet and dry soils. What type of soil is the wettest and driest?

Wet Soils	Dry Soils
Less room for air.	More room for air. The air combines with iron and makes the soil look lighter.
Darker in color.	Lighter/brighter colors.
Contains more humus.	Contain less Humus.
Clay is a wet type of soil.	Sand is one of the driest types of soil.

23. ✔ WR-   After reading page 88, which soil type do you think is best for growing crops? Explain why you think this.

I think wet soils like silt and clay are best for growing crops because they contain more humus and smaller grains of rock. The crops will not need as much water because these soils do not dry out as quickly as sand does.

24. ✔ PP-   Read page 89, 1st sentence of 1st paragraph under "Importance of Soils." Predict what you think the world would be like without soil.

Possible prediction/discussion: If there wasn't any soil in the world, I do not think trees, plants, or foods would be able to grow. If these didn't grow, then animals and humans would not be able to eat, they would go hungry, and eventually die out. Nothing would be able to survive on Earth if soil did not exist.

25. ? RR-   Read page 89, 1st paragraph under "Importance of Soils." Describe what would actually happen if there was no soil in the world.

Possible discussion: People would not be able to make bricks, pottery, or other items made from clay soil. Many animals would have nowhere to live and most plants would not be able to grow.

26. ✔ WR-   Read page 89, 2nd paragraph under "Importance of Soils." Describe what **loam** is. Why do you think loam is usually found on farms?

Loam is the best type of soil to use to grow fruits and vegetables. It is usually found on farms. It is a mixture of humus, clay, silt, and sandy soils. I think loam is usually found on farms because it is the best soil to use when growing crops due to the fact that it has characteristics of all the other types of soil.

27. ✔ WR-   After reading page 89, imagine you started a vegetable garden in an area that has sandy soil. Describe what would happen to the vegetables you planted and why this would happen.

Only a few vegetables would grow and most would die before they were ready to be picked and eaten because sand it not a good soil type to use to grow vegetables. Sandy soils do not hold on to much water and do not contain much humus. These are necessary elements for crops to grow and mature.

28. ✔ DP-   After reading page 89, talk about ways people use different types of soil.

Possible response: People use soils to make pottery, and to plant trees, flowers, gardens, and fruits and vegetables. People also use some soils as fertilizer on farms.

Textbook Activity Guide
Social Studies—4th Grade

Penny Kirkpatrick
Kennesaw State University
"The Struggle for Reforms"—Pages 416–420

Reading Codes:
RST—Read silently by yourself, and think about the answer.
RPA—Read with your partner, and answer the question together.
RPW—Read with your partner, answer the question, and write the answer on paper.
RW—Read on your own, and write the answer on your paper.
RDE—Read on your own, draw a diagram, chart, or map, and write an explanation for it.

Self-Monitoring Codes:

✔ I understood this section.

✗ I did not understand this section.

? I don't know if I understood this section.

Note: Answers are indicated in boxes below each question.

1. ✔ RST. Read the title of the chapter and the first paragraph on page 416. What do you think this section of the chapter will be about?

   I think this section will be about reforms in the United States. I also think I will learn about the first women's rights convention.

2. ✔ RPA. Read the second paragraph on page 416. What do you think the following sentence means: "A spirit of change fills the air here, and throughout the country."

   We think it means that the men and women at the convention are excited because women may finally get some rights like the men have. This convention was the first in history and people were happy about some of the new changes that might happen.

3. ✔ RPW. Read the third paragraph on page 416. According to Elizabeth Cady Stanton, what are the three desired reforms she spoke of in her speech at the convention?

   The three reforms are: declare our right to be free, to be represented in the government, and demand our right to vote.

4. ✔ RW. After reading the last sentence in paragraph three on page 416, do you think her speech inspired people in the United States to promote change? Write two reasons why you agree or disagree.

   I agree that the convention did inspire change in our country. Women can vote, women are represented in government and the military, and women have the same rights as men.

5. ✔ RST. Read the title of the section that begins on page 417. What do you think the title means? What was the Second Great Awakening?

   I think it is the second time a big reform has taken place in the United States. Awakening might mean that people know they need to wake up and see what's happening.

6. ✔ RPA. Read the first paragraph on page 417. What does the phrase "a spirit of reform" mean? Why do you think the people were thinking about religion in their lives?

   It means that people wanted to change things in the United States. Maybe because the people had forgotten about God and living their lives like the Bible says. They knew they were making mistakes in the way they were living their lives, and they wanted to change.

7. __✔__ RPW.   Read the second paragraph on page 417. What are revivals? Why did parts of central and western New York get the nickname of the "Burned-Over District"?

Revivals are big meetings that strengthened peoples' feelings about religion. A preacher, Charles G. Finney, gave long and fiery speeches at the revivals. We looked up the word fiery in the dictionary, and it means burning or scorching. Since Finney's speeches were so hot, that is how the nickname was formed.

8. __✔__ RW.   Read the third paragraph on page 417. How did people believe they could become better and make their country better?

The people thought religion could make them better. If religion could make them better people, and everyone believed in religion, then the whole country would be better too.

9. __?__ RST.   Read the fourth paragraph on page 417. What started the nation's first great era of reform? What are two behaviors that people of that time believed were bad? What was the major crusade to stop people from drinking alcohol called? What does temperance mean and what did people who believe in temperance try to do?

The Second Great Awakening started the nation's first great era of reform. Two behaviors were gambling and drinking alcohol. The major crusade was called the temperance movement. Temperance means moderation, and the people tried to encourage others to drink very little or none at all.

10. __✔__ RPA.   Read the last paragraph on page 417. What were two changes that reformers wanted to see take place?

They wanted to bring an end to slavery and gain rights for women.

11. __✔__ RPW.   Now that you have finished reading the section titled "The Second Great Awakening," how did the awakening lead to the temperance movement?

The awakening was about bringing religion back into the lives of people in the United States. If you have religion in your life, you have better values and avoid things like drinking too much, cussing, gambling, or lying. Since the people wanted to improve their lives, they started the temperance movement to convince other people to live better lives too.

12. __✔__ RW.   Read the first paragraph on page 418, under the heading "Fighting Against Slavery." When and where did anti-slavery groups begin to form? Was John Quincy Adams for or against slavery, and how do you know?

Anti-slavery groups started in the northern part of the United States and started back during the time of the Revolution. Later, in the early 1800s, John Quincy Adams was against slavery because he wrote a poem that said God wants all the slaves to rise until no slave is found on earth.

13. __✔__ RST.   Read the second paragraph on page 418. What are abolitionists, what did they do, and when did they start to form?

Abolitionists were reformers who were against slavery. They started fighting against slavery in the 1830s by giving speeches and writing stories for newspapers.

14. __✔__ RPA.   Read the third paragraph on page 418. Why do you think Frederick Douglass was "a powerful and eloquent voice for the abolitionists?"

Since he used to be a slave, until he escaped, he knew how awful slavery was. He wanted to talk to anybody and everybody how slavery should be stopped.

15. __✔__ RPW.   Read paragraph four on page 418. What are two things that happened to Douglass when he was a slave? Do you think his experiences helped him convince others that slavery is wrong? Why or why not?

Douglass was badly beaten and almost starved to death. Since those things happened to him personally, he could tell people horrible details about what he had to go through. We think what he went through really upset and hurt him, so he got people's attention when he told his stories. What he went through made many people angry enough to want to stop slavery and keep those things from happening to more people.

16. __✔__ RW.   Read the fifth paragraph on page 418. Who was William Lloyd Garrison? What do you think he meant when he said, "I do not wish to think, or speak, or write, with moderation . . . ?" Why do you think he felt this way?

William Lloyd Garrison was an abolitionist who started his own newspaper called *The Liberator*. I think he meant that he was not going to hold anything back in the stories he wrote. He was going to be truthful and write all about the evils of slavery. He hated slavery and wanted people to know the truth about the horrible experiences of slaves. Since he hated slavery so much, he wanted other people to hate it too and help put a stop to it.

17. __✔__ RST.   Read the last paragraph on page 418. Who was Sojourner Truth, and how did she get her name? How did she convince people that slavery was evil?

Sojourner Truth was born into slavery. Later, she escaped and became a preacher. Sojourn means travel, so she wanted to travel everywhere, spreading the truth about the evils of slavery. She convinced people by reading truths from the Bible about how to treat people and how to end slavery.

18. __✔__ RDE.   Now that you have finished reading the section "Fighting Against Slavery," draw a table that contains the following information: name the abolitionist and the method the abolitionist used to spread the message about ending slavery.

Abolitionist	Way Message Was Spread
Frederick Douglass	Speeches
William Lloyd Garrison	Newspaper
Sojourner Truth	Speeches

19. __✔__ RPA.   Read the first paragraph on page 419, under the heading "Women's Rights." Name three things that women were not allowed to do in the early 1800s.

Women could not vote, could not go to most colleges, and they were not allowed to own any property once they were married.

20. __✔__ RPW.   Read the second paragraph on page 419. Name two women who were active reformers, and the reform movements in which they were involved. How do you think the women felt when they went to the London anti-slavery convention?

The two women were Lucretia Mott and Elizabeth Cady Stanton. They fought for women's rights, temperance, and the abolition of slavery. We think they were really angry when they went to the convention, and they were told they were not allowed to speak. It probably upset them so much that they wanted to fight even harder for women's rights and abolition of slavery in the United States.

21. __?__ RW.   Read the third paragraph on page 419. What happened at the Seneca Falls Convention? What was the main idea presented in the declaration?

Elizabeth Stanton presented a Declaration of Sentiments. Her declaration was based on the Declaration of Independence. The main idea was that all men and women are created equal.

22. __✔__ RST.   Read paragraph four on page 419. What are resolutions? Do you think men were as supportive as women for increasing women's rights? Why or why not?

Resolutions are like statements, and these statements are about the rights women should have. I do not think men were as supportive for change as women. I think this because 68 women signed the Declaration, and only 32 men signed it. I think the men did not want things to change because they did not have to suffer like the women. They had no idea how horrible the women felt about their lives.

23. __?__ RPA.   Read the last paragraph on page 419. What did the press think about the Seneca Falls Convention? Did the comments made by the press make Elizabeth Stanton happy or angry? Why?

The press was not in favor of the convention. Reporters made comments like: "A woman is a nobody." They also said that "women were unfit for citizenship." Stanton was not upset by the comments because she thought, "At least the convention is getting some publicity and will hopefully get men and women involved in fighting for women's rights."

24. __✔__ RDE.   Now that you have finished reading the section titled "Women's Rights," draw a table that lists 3 resolutions presented at the convention and what those resolutions mean.

Resolution	Meaning
"All laws which . . . place [woman] in a position inferior to that of man . . . [have] no force or authority."	Any law that says a woman is not as valued/ important (not given the same rights) as a man will not be enforceable/valid.
"Woman is man's equal and was intended to be so by the Creator."	Our Creator, God, created the woman as the man's equal (of the same importance).
"It is the duty of women in this country to secure to themselves their sacred right to elective franchise [the right to vote]."	Women should have the right to vote.

25. __✔__ RPW.   After reading the first paragraph on page 420, under the heading "The Spirit of Reform," name some conditions that reformers thought needed changing in the United States.

They were slavery, women's rights, education, prison living conditions, and treatment of the mentally ill.

26. __?__ RW.   Read the second paragraph on page 420. What were Horace Mann's beliefs about education? What reforms did Mann bring to the public education system?

Horace Mann felt that one needed an education to escape poverty. He also thought that education produced "intelligent and practical men," which led them out of poverty. Mann was able to extend the Massachusetts school year to 6 months, build more high schools, and improve teacher training.

27. __✔__ RST.   After reading the third paragraph on page 420, what institutions did Dorothea Dix visit, and what did she discover during her visits?

Dorothea Dix visited prisons and insane asylums. She discovered that the mentally ill patients were "beaten with rods" and "lashed into obedience."

28. __✔__ RDE.   Now that you have finished reading the entire chapter, create a timeline of the reform movements that took place in the early-mid 1800s.

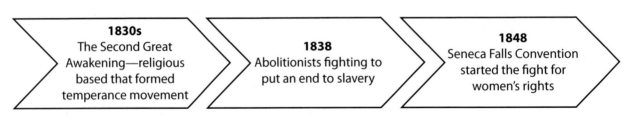

1830s
The Second Great Awakening—religious based that formed temperance movement

1838
Abolitionists fighting to put an end to slavery

1848
Seneca Falls Convention started the fight for women's rights

Textbook Activity Guide (TAG)-Grade 4

Amy Pope
Kennesaw State University
Ecosystems: Chapter 3 Lesson 1

Reading Codes:
RST—Read silently by yourself and think about the answer.
RPA—Read silently with your partner and answer the question together.
RPW—Read with your partner, answer the question, and write the answer on the paper.
RW—Read on your own and write the answer on your paper.
RDE—Read on your own, draw a diagram, chart, or map, and write an explanation for it.
DCM—Complete the diagram, chart or map on your own.

Self-Monitoring Codes:

✔   I understood this section.

✗   I did not understand this section.

?   I don't know if I understood this section.

1. ✔ RST: Read the title of the lesson on page 79, and think about the answer to the question it poses.

   A systems consists of many parts that all work together to make the system function.

2. ✔ RPW: Read the first paragraph on page 79 under the heading *What a System Is*. Why is it important for a system to have all of its parts?

   A system should have all its parts because if a part is missing or damaged, it will not work well, if at all.

3. ✔ RPA: Ecosystems are discussed in the two paragraphs under the heading *Ecosystems* on page 79. What are two ecosystems that can be found around your home or community?

   Examples of two ecosystems that can be found around a home or community are a forest and a dead, rotting tree.

4. ✔ RPW: Read the second paragraph under the heading *Ecosystems* on page 79. List three examples each of living and nonliving parts of a desert ecosystem.

   Answers will vary. Examples of parts of a desert ecosystem: Living- snake, bush, coyote; Nonliving- rock, sand, sunlight.

5. ? RW: On page 80, the paragraph under the heading *Kinds of Ecosystems* discusses how different types of animals and plants survive better than others in a specific environment. Write down an instance where an animal or plant would not be able to survive in a specific ecosystem and tell why. (EX. A tomato plant could not survive in the tundra because it would be too cold.)

   Answers will vary. Examples: A banana tree cannot live in the desert because it needs a lot of water to survive; a polar bear could not survive in a rainforest because its coat would not provide camouflage, and it would not be able to sneak up on prey.

6. ✔ RPA: Read about the adaptation of the Saguaro cactus at the bottom of the paragraph on page 80. How did the cactus adapt to the harsh environment of the desert?

   The Saguaro cactus can expand to fill up with water when it rains, so it can survive in a drought.

7. ___✔___ DCM: Different kinds of ecosystems are discussed in the illustrations on pages 80 and 81. Use this to complete the chart below by filling in details about each type of ecosystem. You do not need to write in complete sentences.

Desert	Grassland	Tundra	Forest	Tropical Rainforest
Driest ecosystem; low amounts of rainfall; organisms include cacti, shrubs, coyotes, and roadrunners	Covered with tall grasses; get medium amounts of rain; organisms include grasshoppers, prairie chickens, and bison	Very cold and dry; ground beneath surface is frozen all year; some grasses grow but no trees; organisms include arctic foxes and caribou	Has many trees, bushes, and wildflowers; a bit more than average rainfall; organisms include deer, foxes, raccoons, and squirrels	Large amounts of rain; many trees and a lot of vegetation; many species of plants and animals; organisms include toucans, monkeys, and orchids

8. ___✗___ RST: The first paragraph under *Organisms and Their Environment* on page 82 describes a population of prairie dogs. If the amount of water decreased in the area where the prairie dogs lived, what do you think would happen to the population?

Student answers will vary. Some include: the prairie dogs will move to find more water; some will die of thirst, etc.

9. ___?___ RPW: Read the second paragraph under *Organisms and Their Environment* on page 82. What is an example of a community and a population in a forest ecosystem?

An example of a community in a forest would be the animals that live in an old hollow tree, and an example of a population would be the members of the squirrel species.

10. ___✔___ RW: Read the third paragraph under *Organisms and Their Environment* on page 82. What is a habitat? What clue are you given to remember what a habitat is?

A habitat is the area or place where an organism lives. You can think of it as the organism's "address."

11. ___?___ DCM: Read the last paragraph on page 82 under the heading *Special Roles*. Fill in the Venn diagram with the Lucifer Hummingbird and the roadrunner. Be sure to label each animal's niche. Underneath the diagram, write your own definition of a niche.

Answers will vary.

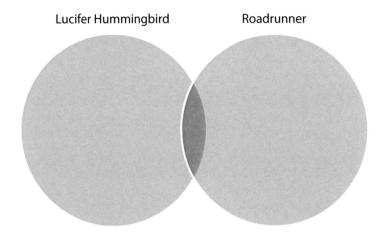

A niche is a small part of a habitat that a specific category of organism lives in.

12. ✔ RPA: Look at the picture of the Lucifer Hummingbird on page 82. How do its physical traits help it fulfill its niche?

The long, slender beak allows it to get nectar and eat insects inside flowers. It can fly, which allows it to avoid predators.

13. ✔ RDE: As a review of the lesson, create a flow chart with the following characteristics: population, community, and ecosystem. List an example of each, but make sure they all fit into the same ecosystem.

Answers will vary.

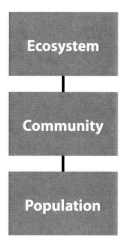

Interactive Reading Guide (Social Studies—Intermediate Level)

Chapter 12: Japan—An Island Country

Interaction codes:

◯ = Individual

◉ = Pairs

◉ = Group

◯ = Whole class

◉ 1. In your group, write down everything you can think of relative to the topics listed below on Japan. Your group's association will then be shared with the class.

```
                        Japan
         location  ⟋  /  |  \  ⟍  major cities
                land  /   |   \  industry
                 seasons  |  products
                        food
```

◯◉ 2. Read page 156 and jot down 5 things about the topography of Japan. Share this information with your partner.

◯ 3. Read to remember all you can about the "Seasons of Japan." The associations of the class will then be written on the board for discussion.

◉ 4. a. Take turns "whisper reading" the three sections under "Feeding the People of Japan." After each section, retell, with the aid of your partner, the information in your own words.
   b. What have you learned about the following?
      terraces, paddies, thresh, other crops, fisheries

◉ 5. Put two pencils together and allow each person in the group to try eating with chopsticks. Discuss your experiences with the group.

◉ 6. With your partner, use your prior knowledge to predict whether the following statements are true or false *before* reading the section on "industrialized Japan." Return to these statements *after* reading to see if you've changed your view. In all cases, be sure to explain your answers. You do not have to agree with your partner.
   a. Japan does not produce its own raw materials but instead gets them from other countries.
   b. Japan is one of the top 10 shipbuilding countries.
   c. Japan makes more cars than the U.S.
   d. Silk used to be produced by silkworms but now it is a manmade fiber.
   e. Silkworms eat mulberry leaves.
   f. The thread from a single cocoon is 600 feet long.

◯◉ 7. After reading, write down 3 new things you learned about the following topics. Compare these responses with those of your group.
   Other industries of Japan
   Old and new ways of living

◯◉ 8. Read the section on "Cities of Japan." Each group member is to choose a city, show its location on the map in the textbook, and report on some facts about it.

◯◯ 9. Return to the major topics introduced in the first activity. Skim over your chapter reading guide responses with these topics in mind. Next, be ready to contribute, along with the class, anything you have learned about these topics.

Analogical Strategy Guide for Intermediate-Level Science Lesson

Element of Circulatory System	Picture	Function	Similar Element of Road System	Picture
Red Blood Cells		Carry gases to and from the body's cells	Cars	
Hemoglobin		Protein that carries oxygen to the body	Gasoline	
Bone Marrow		Makes red blood cells	Car factories and dealers	
White Blood Cells		Fight diseases and infections	Traffic cop	
Platelets		Produce blood clots that stop the bleeding	Construction barrier	
Arteries		Carry blood away from the heart	Highways	
Veins		Carry blood to the heart	Numbered routes (more rural than highway)	
Capillaries		Connect arteries to veins	Exit ramp off freeway	
Heart		Muscular organ that pumps blood to the body	City	

Wood, K. D., Lapp, D., Flood, J., & Taylor, D. B. (2008). *Guiding readers through text: Strategy guides for new times.* Newark, DE: International Reading Association. (pg. 125).
From "Interactive Reading Guide" by Wood, K. D., Lapp, D., and Flood, J., in *Guiding Readers Through Text: A Review of Study Guides.* Copyright © 2008 by the International Reading Association (www.reading.org). Reproduced with permission of International Reading Association via Copyright Clearance Center.

Strategies for Note Taking and Study Skills

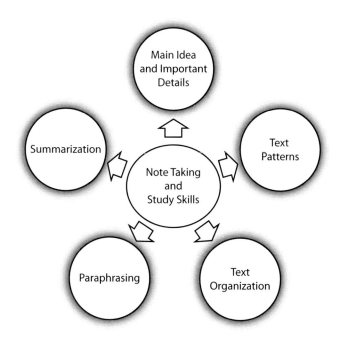

The note taking strategies presented in Chapter Four demonstrate ways teachers can help students learn how to identify and record main ideas and important details from informational text in order to paraphrase the information in their own words. Through a process that teaches children how to paraphrase and summarize, students are presented with effective note taking strategies they can take with them beyond their middle and high school years. In addition, this chapter presents useful study skills based on research conducted on taking standardized tests and answering essay questions. Research conducted by literacy experts, such as Hoffman (1992); Caverly, Mandeville, and Nicholson (1995); and Anderson and Pearson (1984) have informed literacy practice for comprehension instruction and teaching research and study skills in classrooms across the nation and the world. These strategies will have a positive impact on student achievement by helping students to become effective independent learners.

SNAP! Notes! Simple Notes Are Perfect! (It's a Snap!)

First Experience for Making Notes (Grades 2–5)

As a first time fourth grade teacher, I learned very early my first year that my fourth graders did not know how to paraphrase, or put what they have read in their own words. They tended to copy everything word for word out of encyclopedias, trade books, and other sources, which they found when writing reports on assigned topics. I knew that I needed to find a way to support my students' development of identifying main ideas and important details, nurturing their skills in summarization, and promoting their development as writers of informational text. Since students do not learn these skills on their own, they must be systematically taught through think-alouds and scaffolding. It is important to provide numerous opportunities for students to practice in whole class, small groups, and with partners before attempting to apply these strategies and skills independently.

After exploring the research literature and brainstorming, I began utilizing this simple approach during whole class instruction to demonstrate how to read a small chunk of text and cover it up. First I ask, "What does this mostly talk about?" Students answer the question in a one word or short phrase format to supply the main idea of the small chunk of text. Next, I ask "What does it say about (the main idea)?" Here, students write one word or a short phrase to supply details about the main idea. Using the format explained below, after the text is read and notes are written, I return to the first box of information and ask students, as a group, to compose a sentence or two to summarize their notes for the main idea and details in each box. Then we return to the first box reserved for the introductory sentence or paragraph and compose the introductory paragraph as a class. Finally, students return to the last box and compose a summary paragraph. In the end, students take notes in their own words and compose a six or more paragraph report on the topic, which is based on one source of information.

Alice

Procedures for Using SNAP! Notes:

- First, demonstrate to students how to fold paper (I often use construction paper) into **four, six**, or **eight squares**, depending on the number of pages, paragraphs, or sections in a text you want them to read. The back side of the paper may also be used if needed.
- Next, ask students to number each box as shown below and on the example on the next page. Reserve the first and last squares for introductory and summary sentences or paragraphs, depending on the grade level. Each numbered box represents a page, section, or paragraph of the text.
- Then, ask students to *silently* read a page, section, or paragraph of text. Then they cover it up or turn it over when they are finished.
- After reading, ask students to write notes in *their own words* from the text in the corresponding boxes, to answer, "What does the paragraph, section, or page mostly talk about (main idea)?" Then ask, "What does it say about it?"
- Next, from the notes, students formulate their own paragraphs. For younger students, they write one big paragraph if each box is one sentence long. For older elementary students, they may write six or more paragraphs, depending on the length of the text they have read.
- Then, they compose an *introductory paragraph* in the first box and a *summary paragraph* in the last box.
- Finally, they may create a report on the topic with an introductory paragraph, followed by two, three, or more supporting paragraphs, and ending with a summary paragraph.

Boxes are numbered accordingly:

1   Keep **Box 1** blank for **introductory** sentence or paragraph.

2   In **Box 2**, answer the question, "What does the **first** paragraph, section, or page mostly talk about?" (main idea)—"What does it say about it?" (details)- Students write short phrases, single word details.

3   In **Box 3**, answer the question, "What does the **second** paragraph, section, or page mostly talk about?" (main idea)—"What does it say about it?" (details)- Students write short phrases, single word details.

4   In **Box 4**, answer the question, "What does the **third** paragraph, section, or page mostly talk about?" (main idea)—"What does it say about it?" (details)-Students write short phrases, single word details.

5   In **Box 5**, answer the question, "What does the **fourth** paragraph, section, or page mostly talk about?" (main idea)—"What does it say about it?" (details) [Continue with boxes until end of assigned reading].

6   Keep **Box 6** (or the last box) blank for **summary** sentence or paragraph.

*See next page for sample SNAP! Notes! format.

SNAP! Notes!—Simple Notes Are Perfect! (It's a Snap!)

1 Keep this box blank for **introductory** sentence or paragraph.	**2** What does the **first** paragraph, section, or page mostly talk about? (main idea) ▪ What does it say about it? (details)	**3** What does the **second** paragraph, section, or page mostly talk about? (main idea) ▪ What does it say about it? (details)
4 What does the **third** paragraph, section, or page mostly talk about? (main idea) ▪ What does it say about it? (details)	**5** What does the **fourth** paragraph, section, or page mostly talk about? (main idea) ▪ What does it say about it? (details)	**6** Keep this box blank for **summary** sentence or paragraph.

Herringbone Technique

The **Herringbone Technique**, developed by Herber (1978), is a structured outline used to help students in grades 3–12 focus on specific information in a content area or non-fiction text while assisting them with organizing the information by answering six basic questions: Who? What? When? Where? Why? and How? The teacher provides the Herringbone outline on which the student gleans information from the text and records the information on the outline to answer the six basic questions. After completing the Herringbone, the student writes a summary of the recorded information in his/her own words. As a result, the Herringbone Technique enables students to recall information presented in the text or chapter. Once completed, students may use the Herringbone for writing reports and studying.

Herringbone Activity

Topic: _____

Name: _____   Partner(s): _____

1. Read the assigned chapter or selection and fill in the outline below.

2. Write a summary below of the information you recorded on the outline.

_____
_____
_____
_____
_____
_____

Adapted from: Herber, H. L. (1978). Teaching reading in content areas. (2nd ed.). In K. D. Wood & D. Bruce Taylor (Eds.), *Literacy strategies across the subject areas: Process-oriented blackline masters for the K-12 classroom* (pp. 71–74). Boston, MA: Pearson.

Two-Column Note Taking

Two-Column Note Taking is an effective method of taking notes from reading informational text that serves as an effective transition from the SNAP Notes approach. Based on Pauk's Cornell Note Taking method (1974), it provides an efficient, flexible alternative to the more traditional, rigid, outline format. Students may be introduced to the Two-Column approach after mastering the SNAP Notes method, which supports paraphrasing and note taking with single words and short phrases. Although Two-Column Note Taking may be used for notes during lectures in grades 7–12 and college, in grades 4–6, it is best used to support recording information that is being read. After notes are recorded for assigned readings, Two-Column Notes make excellent study tools. In addition, the written summaries at the bottom of each page of notes may be used for writing reports or research papers because they are in the student's own words. The steps for students to create **Two-Column Notes** are as follows:

Step One: Fold a sheet of notebook paper in half. At the top, write the **chapter title or lesson title and page number(s)** that you will be reading and recording notes for on the sheet.

Step Two: Under the chapter/lesson title and page number, at the top of the left side column, write **Question or Category**. At the top of the right-side column, write **Text Notes**. Draw a line down the center to separate the two columns, but leave about **two inches at the bottom.**

Step Three: At the bottom, write **Summary (in my own words)**: Fold your paper in half at the line. Look at the right-hand column under **Text Notes.**

Step Four: Now, begin reading the assigned pages/lesson/chapter. As you read, **write/record** the heading titles under **Text Notes**, and any important information, in short words or phrases, under each heading. Be careful not to copy full sentences from the text. Once you have filled the right side of the page with your notes, stop and go back to the top of the page and readjust the page numbers you wrote. Only write the page number(s) for the actual page(s) for the notes on each sheet.

Step Five: Next, look at the left-hand column under **Question or Category**. Directly across from the top to the right, look at the information you wrote, and think about a **question** you could ask that can be answered from the information you wrote. You may also think of a **category or concept** the information relates to. Write the **question or category** on the left-side column that relates to the information on the right. Continue to do this for each section of information you wrote on the right side of the paper, making sure your **question or category** is written directly across from the corresponding information on the right.

Step Six: At the bottom, under the **Summary (in my own words)**, write a summary of the notes you took on the right-side column. Be sure the summary is in your own words.

Step Seven: Begin a new page of notes as you continue to read and take notes until all notes are recorded for the assigned text reading. Be sure to set up each page in the two-column format.

Step Eight: After all notes are recorded, questions or categories are written, and summaries are written, you may use your two-column notes as study tools by folding your notes in half, revealing only the left-side column of **Question or Category**. As you read each question or category, recite the answer. Then look on the right-side column's **Text Notes** to check to see if your answer is correct.

Adapted from: Pauk, W. (1974). *How to study in college*. Boston, MA: Houghton Mifflin.

Richardson, J. S., Morgan, R. F., & Fleener, C. (2006). *Reading to learn in the content areas*. (6th ed.). Belmont, CA: Thomson/Wadsworth.

The Best Book of Fossils, Rocks, and Minerals

Pages 6 and 7

Question or Category	Text Notes
What are the three types of rocks?	Our Rocky World *three types of rocks ■ Sedimentary ■ Igneous ■ Metamorphic
How are surface rocks named?	*Rocks named based on how they are formed
How are igneous rocks formed?	■ By fire-igneous-lava from volcanoes ■ crust is hard/rocky ■ core is hot solid & liquid metal
What makes up sedimentary rock?	■ Layers of sediment 　■ sand, shells, clay pressed hard together
How are metamorphic rocks formed?	■ Changed rocks 　■ metamorphic—heat & pressure then pushed up from underground 　■ forms mountains, hills

Summary (in my own words): There are three types of rocks, igneous, sedimentary, and metamorphic. They get their names by how they are formed. Igneous rocks are formed by fire from lava coming out of volcanoes which then cools and hardens. Sedimentary rock is formed by layers of sand, shells, and clay that get pressed down together. Metamorphic rock gets changed by heat and pressure which pushes it up from under the surface of the earth. It forms mountains and hills.

Pellant, C. (2000). *The best book of fossils, rocks, and minerals.* New York, NY: Kingfisher Publications.
Adapted from: Pauk, W. (1974). *How to study in college.* Boston, MA: Houghton Mifflin.
Richardson, J. S., Morgan, R. F., & Fleener, C. (2006). *Reading to learn in the content areas.* (6th ed.). Belmont, CA: Thomson/Wadsworth.

Two-Column Note Taking

Chapter _____   Page(s) _____

Question or Category	Text Notes

Summary (in my own words): _____

_____

_____

_____

_____

PLAN Note Taking

A One-Page Graphic Organizer for Taking Notes

PLAN is a research-based, note taking and study strategy designed to promote active reading before, during, and after reading while developing a reader's ability to identify main ideas and key details from expository texts. The reader associates these ideas and details with schemata and prior knowledge, recording them on a map or diagram in short phrases or single word notations. PLAN asks students to develop their graphic organizer based on the organizational structure of the text. Developed originally for middle school through college level learners by Caverly, Mandeville, and Nicholson (1995), PLAN can be effectively implemented with fourth and fifth graders after they have learned to take notes using the SNAP Notes method in which they learn to identify main ideas and key details, write them in one-word or short phrases, and paraphrase their notes through written summaries. The process for implementing PLAN is described below:

Predict: **Predict** the content and structure of the text to assess its potential for the reading task or purpose. Create a skeleton MAP or DIAGRAM with chapter title at center, and subtitles (subheadings) highlighted words, and information from graphics as **major** and **minor** branches. (This step reflects the comprehension strategy of *prediction*.) [See **Step One: Predict** for example].

Locate: **Locate** known and unknown information on the map *from your background knowledge*, in other words, what do you already know about each of the headings, words, etc? Place a check (✔) by information you know or are familiar with and a (?) next to information you are not familiar with. (This step reflects the comprehension strategy of assessing **prior knowledge of content.**) [See **Step Two: Locate** for example].

Add: Add words and short phrases to the map *while reading* to explain concepts marked with a (?) and confirm or add information marked with a (✔). This step reflects the **metacognitive** nature of constructing understanding/comprehension in the reading process. In addition, students are encouraged to use **fix-up strategies** if they do not understand concepts, such as rereading, using the dictionary or glossary for confusing words, or dismissing a point to revisit it a later time. This step is crucial to content recall and application. [See **Step Three: Add** for example].

Note: Take note of new understanding and use it to fulfill your task. Use your completed map or diagram as a study tool. Take note of what you learned from your reading. You might (1) reproduce your map by memory, or (2) write a summary of your map. [See **Step Four: Note** for example].

Adapted from: Caverly, D. C., Mandeville, T. F., & Nicholson, S. A. (1995). PLAN: A study-reading strategy for informational text. *Journal of Adolescent and Adult Literacy, 39*(3), 190–199.

Sample PLAN Method of Note Taking with 4th Grade Science Textbook

STEP ONE—PREDICT (predict structure of text by previewing, making a skeleton map of the section headings, and words in bold print or italics).

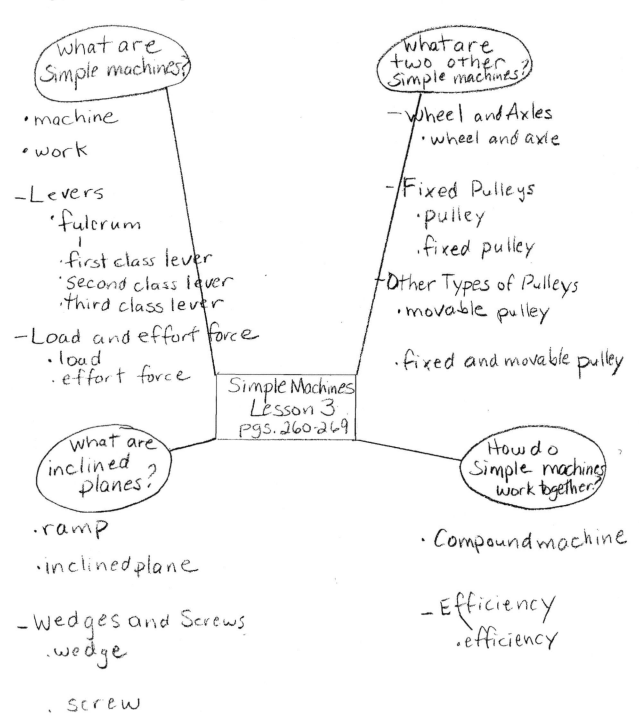

Sample PLAN Method of Note Taking with 4th Grade Science Textbook

STEP TWO—LOCATE (Assess background knowledge about what you already know. Put check marks by the things you know and question marks by the things you do not know BEFORE you read).

What are Simple machines?

- machine ✓
- work ✓
- simple machine ?
- Levers ?
  - fulcrum ?
    - first class lever ?
    - second class lever ?
    - third class lever ?
- Load and effort force ?
  - load ✓
  - effort force ?

What are two other Simple machines?

- Wheel and Axles
  - wheel and axle ?
- Fixed Pulleys ?
  - pulley ?
  - fixed pulley ?
- Other Types of Pulleys
  - movable pulley ?
  - fixed and movable pulley !

Simple Machines
Lesson 3
pgs. 260-269

What are inclined planes?

- ramp ?
- inclined plane ?
- wedges and screws
  - wedge ?
  - screw ✓

How do simple machines work together?

- Compound machines,
- Efficiency ?
  - efficiency ?

Sample PLAN Method of Note Taking
with 4th Grade Science Textbook

STEP 3—ADD (add additional information while you READ by writing short phrases by the things you know (to enhance what you know) and the things you do not know).

Center box: Simple Machines Lesson 3 pgs 260-269

what are Simple machines?
- machine ✓ - helps us do work
- work ✓ - happens when force is used to move an object
- simple machine ? - has only a few parts
- Levers ? - SM w/ only 2 parts (bar + fulcrum)
  - fulcrum ? - part that supports bar - allows it to turn + pivot
  - first class lever ? - fulcrum b/t load + effort force
  - second class lever ? - fulcrum at end + load in middle
  - third class lever ? - fulcrum at end + effort force in middle
- Load and Effort Force
  - load ✓ - object being moved by lever
  - effort force ? - force used to do work

what are two other simple machines?
- wheel and Axles ? - has 2 parts
  - wheel and axle ? - bar that passes through center of wheel
- Fixed Pulleys?
  - pulley?
  - fixed pulley ? - wheel is attached to something - can't change position
  - changes direction on a force
- Other Types of Pulleys
  - movable pulley ? - not attached to a fixed object - moves same direction as load
  - fixed and movable pulley? - combo of 2 pulleys - effort force less than movable pulley + is opposite direction of moving load

what are inclined planes?
- ramp ? - inclined plane - a 1-part simple machine w/ a flat slanted surface
- inclined plane ? - flat slanted surface w/ one simple part - needs only small effort
- Wedge and Screws
  - wedge ? - SM - changes downward force or forward force into a sideways force
  - screw ✓ - inclined plane twisted into a spiral
  - wedges + screws trade distance for effort force

How do simple machines work together?
- compound machine ? - 2 or more simple machines together
- Efficiency ? - friction reduces efficiency
  - efficiency ? - how much work a machine produces compared to amount of work applied
- Scissors - wedge, fulcrum
- nut cracker - fulcrum
- doorknob - wheel + axle
- bicycle - lever, wheel, axle, screw

Sample PLAN Method of Note Taking
with 4th Grade Science Textbook

STEP 4—NOTE (Make note of what you have learned by either re-creating the map completely by memory or by writing a summary of the map by memory).

The end result of the PLAN map is a good device for studying for tests as well as for organizing and writing reports. Just include an introductory paragraph and summary/conclusion paragraph.

Simple machines are anything that helps people do work that are made up of a few parts. Levers are simple machines. They are made up of a bar and a fulcrum. The fulcrum supports the bar and lets it turn or pivot. Levers help us lift heavy things

Wheels and axles are simple machines. An axle is a bar that goes through the center of a wheel. A pulley is a simple machine. It can be a fixed pulley that can't change position but can change direction of a force. It can be a movable pulley that's not attached to a fixed object and it moves the same direction as the load.

Inclined planes are flat slanted surfaces, like a ramp, with one part. Wedges and screws are simple machines, too. Screws are inclined planes twisted into a spiral.

Simple machines can work together. Some simple machines that are made up of 2 or more simple machines are scissors, doornobs, and bicycles.

Inquiry Charts (I-Charts)

Inquiry charts are effective organizers designed to promote critical reading and thinking of informational texts by having students explore a variety of sources of information. I-Charts, developed by James V. Hoffman (1992), are based on the notion that critical thinking skills are nurtured through careful use of strategies that often provide opportunities for children to interact with their peers as they gather and organize information. I-Charts require students to summarize, compare, analyze, and evaluate information they read from multiple forms of text, including books, journals, the Internet, and other media sources. In addition, I-Charts may be utilized in combination with other sources of information, such as experiments, field trips, guest speakers, surveys, and interviews. Inquiry charts may be used in grades 1–12. The process should first be done as a whole class. Once students understand the process, they are ready to use I-Charts on their own. Steps for implementing I-Charts are as follows:

Step One: Decide on the **topic** for exploration and a set of **4–5 guiding questions** you want students to investigate and answer. Encourage students to generate questions for exploration. Construct the I-Chart as per the blank example on the next page, with the **4–5 Guiding Questions** across the top, along with a column for **Interesting Facts and Figures** and **New Questions** students may come up with in the course of their research.

Step Two: Complete the construction of the I-Chart, listing the **Topic, What We Know,** and at least 4 different **Sources** you would like students to use to gather information on the topic down the left side of the chart. The last box is labeled **Summary.**

Step Three: Introduce the I-Chart by first discussing what students already know about the topic and what they will learn or have learned so far. They list any prior knowledge about the topic in the row next to **What We Know,** under any **Guiding Question** their prior knowledge may address. This allows students to see how the I-Chart helps them organize their knowledge about the topic, which will then show them how to organize new information gathered from additional sources while the **Guiding Questions** are answered.

Step Four: Students may work individually, in pairs, or in small groups to search the various sources for information related to the topic in order to answer each of the **Guiding Questions.** Another option for using I-Charts might be to assign different groups to explore one specific **Source.**

Step Five: Once students have completed their I-Charts, they synthesize the information by writing **summary** sentences at the bottom of each column to address the **Guiding Questions.** As their summarization skills become more proficient, they may work in pairs or individually to expand their summaries into paragraphs and written reports.

Step Six: Students compare their new information with their prior knowledge and resolve any misconceptions they may have had prior to their investigations.

Adapted from: Hoffman, J. V. (1992). Critical reading/thinking across the curriculum: Using I-Charts to support learning. In K. D. Wood & D. Bruce Taylor (Eds.), *Literacy strategies across the subject areas: Blackline masters for the K–12 classroom* (pp. 51–53). Boston, MA: Pearson.

I-Chart Form

	Guiding Question	Guiding Question	Guiding Question	Guiding Question		
Topic	1.	2.	3.	4.	Interesting facts and figures	New questions
What we know						
Source 1:						
Source 2:						
Source 3:						
Source 4:						
Summary Statement						

Mnemonic Devices

A **mnemonic device** is an aid used to remember information placed in the form of a rhyme, acronym, or catchy phrase. A mnemonic is a memorable phrase that facilitates recall of information that can be listed using the initial letter from each word. Mnemonics are based on the idea that we learn concepts and labels or names by grouping them in ways that are more easily memorized and recalled. They help students learn specific information and study for tests effectively.

Example mnemonic devices:

Roy G. Biv (primary colors—colors of the rainbow)—red, orange, yellow, green, blue, indigo, and violet

My Very Elegant Mother Just Served Us Nectarines (the eight planets)—Mercury, Venus, Earth, Mars, Jupiter, Saturn, Uranus, and Neptune

HOMES (the five Great Lakes)—Huron, Ontario, Michigan, Erie, and Superior

Please Excuse My Dear Aunt Sally (Parentheses, Exponents, Multiplication/Division, Addition/Subtraction)—order of mathematical operations

King Philip Came Over For Good Soup (phylum, class, order, family, genus, and species)—levels of classification in the Linnaeus naming system

Every Good Boy Does Fine (EGBDF)—lines of the treble clef

Jane Found Michael And Martin Juggling Jellybeans And Skittles Outside Nelly's Door (the months of the year in order)

Days in the Months
Thirty days hath September
April, June and November.
All the rest have thirty-one,
But February, it is great
And brings to us twenty-eight,
Unless it steps out of line
And brings to us twenty-nine (leap year occurs every four years).

Strategies for Test Taking

Many children find taking tests challenging because they just do not know how to approach the test strategically. They may know the content well, but find it difficult to demonstrate their knowledge based on the type of test questions that are presented. Teachers may help all students develop confidence when taking both objective and subjective types of tests by conveying some basic strategies for test taking that children may use for years to come.

Tips for Taking Multiple Choice Tests

☐ Read all choices carefully. *Carefully* is the operative word here!

☐ In a math question, the two numerical extremes, such as highest and lowest, tend to be the wrong answers.

☐ Usually, an answer choice that is the longest tends to be correct.

☐ If you are certain that at least two answers are correct, then choose "all of the above."

☐ Beware of negative words in the instructions or stem of the question. Ask yourself, "What is the question asking?"

☐ Watch out for choices that use the exact words that appear in the passage. They can trick you into choosing the incorrect answer!

☐ Eliminate the one or two obviously *incorrect* answers! Reduce the choices to increase your chances to 50% for choosing the correct answer!

Tips for Taking Other Objective Types of Tests

☐ In a Fill-in-the-Blank question, consider what part of speech is needed to complete the statement. Adjectives or articles, such as *a, an,* or *the,* may indicate that a noun is needed to complete the blank. Check to see what type of word immediately precedes or follows the blank. Always reread the completed sentence to see if it makes sense.

☐ For TRUE/FALSE questions, absolute words used in the answer choices tend to make the response *incorrect* (always, never, none, all). Words like *usually, often, sometimes,* and *generally,* tend to make the response *correct.* Remember, a statement **must** be completely *true* to be *true!*

Tips for Taking Subjective Types of Tests

☐ When answering an essay question, you must first read the question carefully to find out what the question is asking. Be sure to follow the **directions** stated in the question. Then look closely at the **verb(s)** used to determine what the question is asking you to do.

☐ Common verbs used in subjective questions and what each verb requires (asks you to do):

Verb	Task Required for Responding to Question
Analyze	Break the subject into parts, and discuss each part.
Approximate, estimate	Make a reasonable guess in your discussion.
Characterize, explain, describe, identify	Name the characteristics/features that make something/someone special.
Examine	Look carefully at similar answers because one will be a better choice than the others.
Put in chronological order	List events in time order from earliest to latest.
Comment	Give your opinion/point of view and support it with facts/examples.
Compare	Tell how two or more things are similar. Sometimes tell how they are different as well.
Contrast	Tell how two or more things are different.
Discuss	Tell all you can about the topic.
Evaluate	Give evidence on each side of an issue, draw a conclusion from the evidence, and make a judgment about the topic based on the evidence.
Interpret	Explain the meaning of the given topic/idea as you perceive it.
Justify	Provide evidence to support your answer/response.
Name, list, mention	List the information that is asked for in the question without discussion.
Rank	List the information that is asked for in a special order, such as order of importance or chronological order.
State	Give a short, simple answer in which no discussion is necessary.
Summarize	Briefly restate the passage by including the main points and leaving out small details. The answer should be shorter than the original passage.
Trace	Give major points in chronological order.

Adapted from: Frey, N., & Fisher, D. (2007). *Reading for information in elementary school: Content literacy strategies to build comprehension.* Upper Saddle River, NJ: Pearson, Merrill-Prentice Hall.

Writing in the Content Areas

Chapter Five discusses the connections between reading and writing in the content areas and the role writing plays in facilitating what children learn through reading informational texts. Groundbreaking research on writing development in young children conducted by Donald Graves (1983) and Lucy Calkins (1986, 1994) laid the groundwork for writing process and writing workshop that teachers across the country are implementing in their classrooms. In addition, research on the complementary relationship between reading and writing is well documented, especially in relation to writing to learn in the content areas. Experts on writing development (Hansen, 2001; Langer & Applebee, 1987) have provided the foundation for exploring research-based strategies for teaching writing across the curriculum and considering the ways writing promotes reading comprehension and learning from expository texts. This chapter provides a variety of strategies and instructional practices teachers can use to promote writing to learn and writing to show learning while fostering the writing development of their students in grades K–8.

Learning to Write and Writing to Learn

Learning to write begins at a very young age. A child's first attempt at writing is usually demonstrated when taking a crayon and scribbling on any surface that is immediately available. As the child develops as a writer, s/he learns to write letters of the alphabet, encode words, spell (using invented, or temporary, spelling at first), construct sentences, determine how to put sentences together to write a coherent paragraph, and combine paragraphs to write focused reports and essays. Throughout the learning to write process, the student develops an understanding of grammar and the mechanics of writing. Learning to write involves a process which includes prewriting, drafting, revising, editing, and publishing a final written product.

Writing to learn, on the other hand does not involve a process that requires multiple steps necessary to reach a final, refined product. Writing to learn provides opportunities for students to "recall, clarify, and question what they know and what they still wonder about" (Frey & Fisher, 2007, pg. 220). Writing to learn is often used to activate background knowledge and to scaffold conceptual understanding. Writing to learn provides teachers the means to determine what students comprehend about the material they are learning. When completing a writing to learn activity, students must think about and find the words needed to explain what they are learning, how they are making sense of it along the way, and what processes they are using to learn the information. In addition, writing to learn is metacognitive in nature, as it provides the opportunity for students to discover what they do not know about the topic, issue, or themselves as they communicate their knowledge to specific audiences (Jenkinson, 1988, as cited in Frey & Fisher, 2007). Writing tasks are brief, and what is written is not revised or corrected for grammar and mechanics of writing.

Writing to learn requires students to use various kinds of knowledge, depending on the context of the learning situation. Based on research in cognition (Paris, Cross, & Lipson, 1984), there are three kinds of knowledge. **Declarative knowledge** relates to things that we *know,* such as names, facts, labels, and lists. Declarative knowledge is the easiest type of knowledge to disseminate, yet it is important knowledge to convey to students. Declarative knowledge asks *"What?"* and is conveyed through lectures, reading in texts, and through writing to learn prompts, such as quickwrites and brainstorming to determine students' background knowledge about a topic or concept. **Procedural knowledge** refers to knowledge about how to do something or how to apply knowledge in specific ways. Procedural knowledge is more difficult to disseminate through lectures and textbook reading. Instead, students must be given experiences to put procedural knowledge into practice. Procedural knowledge asks *"How?"* and is conveyed through writing to learn prompts such as "How does . . . ?" or "How to . . . ." Another prompt may be "Describe the steps . . . . " **Conditional knowledge** deals with when or why something is done. In other words, it emphasizes the various conditions that influence one's decisions to use knowledge. It relates to the strategies one uses and when to use them. Conditional knowledge asks *"When?"* and *"Why?"* as a means to engage learners to interact with information being presented. Two examples of effective writing to learn prompts that promote conditional knowledge are case studies and scenarios that students can read and respond to in creative ways.

The Impact of Writing Workshop on a Child's Future

It is important for teachers to convey the value of emergent writers' interests and imaginary explorations as they provide writing opportunities in the classroom. These early reading and writing experiences may have a significant impact on a child's future decisions. We will focus on Noelle's writing experiences to illustrate how her development as a writer was nurtured through a writing workshop format in the elementary grades. It is evident from the writing examples on the following pages that Noelle was always intrigued by horses. As a two-year-old, she experienced her first horseback ride which set the stage for her life-long interest, both personally and professionally.

Noelle's teachers nurtured her enthusiasm for horses which manifested in her writing and reading. Through writer's workshop, teachers promoted Noelle's enjoyment of writing by giving her opportunities to express her love of horses. During writing workshop, Noelle's experiences in writing reflected her experiences in play. For example, when Noelle was four, she spent the weekend with a friend, and both children stayed in character "as horses" during the entire weekend, eating, whinnying, and galloping on all fours! In kindergarten, Noelle's writing actually became an extension of that experience and every opportunity she had to be with horses.

Writing was not just a part of writing workshop in Noelle's early elementary grade experiences. Her teachers started each day with free writing in journals. As soon as students arrived, they had opportunities to express their thoughts. When you look at the examples on the following pages, note the characteristics from Noelle's journal entries that align with the Blackburn-Cramp Developmental Writing Scale. What did Noelle understand about language in each example taken from her first grade year in school? What stage of writing development would you designate for each of these examples? How did her writing develop over time from September 9th to February 21st? Based on what you know about first graders' writing development, what do you consider the strengths of Noelle's writing and what areas would you work on to enhance her writing development?

Example 1: Journal sample from week two of the school year
Example 2: Journal sample from week six of the school year
Example 3: Journal sample from the sixth month of the school year

As Noelle grew and continued her development as a writer, she began to explore different genres of writing; however, her topics usually remained the same. In fourth grade, as Noelle continued to write stories about horses, she kept a separate journal of horse diaries in which the horses introduced themselves and told about their experiences. In these entries, it was evident that Noelle's teacher encouraged her to use her imagination to connect the experiences of the horses with her own experiences and knowledge gained from reading.

Example 4: Samples from a Fourth Grader's "Horse Diaries" Journal

Additionally, she began to use writing as a means to understand math, a subject that often presented challenges for her. On her own volition, Noelle began to convert her math problems into story problems as a means to make them more understandable. By doing so, she was able to solve the problems. Her fourth grade teacher was so amazed by this innovation that she copied Noelle's story problems and gave them to all the students to solve. Her fourth grade teacher said that she expected to see Noelle's name on the covers of children's books in the future.

In middle school, she began to write poetry, delving into more thought-provoking issues associated with horses and horse ownership. As an assignment, she wrote an informational piece about an issue that was near and dear to her heart. She chose to write about the plight of unwanted horses by conveying the information from her research through a profound poem. She took the perspectives of three horses as they were being transported to a slaughter house. The poem is presented as Noelle wrote it in seventh grade.

Example 5: Sample of writing to learn through poetry in the middle grades

Noelle actually majored in Equine Business in college, with a minor in creative writing. Now she enjoys working with her own horse and training other young horse enthusiasts to ride as well! Since Noelle experienced the writing process through the writing workshop model throughout her elementary years, she understood what it meant to be a writer and what it took to maintain her own writing. She is currently writing her memoirs!

Samples from a Fourth Grader's "Horse Diaries" Journal

Romeo

Hi! I'm Romeo. I'm 5 years old. I am a honey-colored chestnut stallion. Sierra and Magic and I were brought in from the wild. Here at Noelle's, I fell in love with Juliet's Satin Sapphire, or Juliet, for short. Since I love her so much Noelle decided to call me Romeo, after the play "Romeo and Juliet." I'm not ridden much by Noelle, and we just gallop along the trails so I don't get fat, but she never lets the kids ride me, even the most advanced kids. Everyone says since I'm so beautiful, I should be like a dream to ride. Well, they're wrong! My show name is 'Montegue's Man.'

Juliet's Satin Sapphire

I'm Juliet, short for Juliet's Satin Sapphire. I'm 10 years old. I'm a sorrel with a flaxen mane. When I came to Noelle's, there was only one other horse. That was Goldilocks. We came immediate friends. I was like a 2nd mother to her filly, Golden Love. Soon other horses came. Chapparel, then the mustangs. Romeo is my love. We used to be inseparable, but Noelle put Romeo in the other pasture just a few days ago.

Native Diver

My name is Native Diver. I'm a 7 year old black thoroughbred stallion. I used to be a champion race horse. I was retired and sent to Noelle's when I was 5. She's taken very good care of me. Noelle knew one thing I wanted to do was run. So she would gallop me on the trails. But last year, I hadn't even been at Noelle's for a year, I fell and hurt my leg. The vet fixed it and said I should be OK. Well one day I was running, I stumbled and broke the injured leg. The vet fixed it again but he said no more running! I was devastated! I wanted to run! That's what I was made to do! So you can no longer see me racing up and down the fence line, but you can see me grazing peacefully amongst my many friends. People gave me a ceremony. I have a plaque on the fence that says 'Where the black streak ran.' My show name is 'Hangin by a Thread.'

Reproduced as written by Noelle Snyder, age 9–10.

Example of Writing to Learn/Writing to Show Learning

A Horse's Hell
by Noelle Snyder

Shadow's Magic was a mighty steed
A horse of grace, beauty, and great speed.
One day this great racehorse lost a race
A greater horror would he soon face.

Casper was a sweet old one
A pony that was so much fun.
A faithful family friend, forgotten and unused
Left this poor thing lonely and confused.

Awesome was a champion at heart
He could run, jump and pull a cart.
Awesome's name fit him well
Who knew his life would end in hell?

All three horses met face to face
All with the same fate, going to the same place.
Crammed on a truck with fifty others
Old horses, young horses, foals with no mothers.

Once on the truck, began their journey to hell
One by one they slipped on the floor and fell.
Shadow and another stallion started to fight
Not out of anger, but out of fright.

The truck soon halted to a stop
The drivers came then with cattle prods and crops.
They shoved their weapons through side holes to quiet their cries
They clubbed a few in the head; Casper lost an eye.

Awesome lost his balance and down he fell
Bringing two others with him as well.
Awesome was the perfect horse, over jumps could he fly
He lay his head down, and an hour later he died.

At last, finally! Their death trip was done.
Perhaps now they could get out and run.
Three days with nothing to drink or eat.
Three days of being clubbed, poked, and beat.

Thirty-two horses were already dead.
They were dragged off. The others were led.
Casper was the first to go through
Though he didn't know where he was going to.
They clubbed him in the head and bashed him in the legs.
Down he fell. He crumbled like eggs.

"To be a perfect pony, I did everything I could.
If I could go back and say I'm sorry, I would.
I always listened. I was never bad.
What did I do to make them so very mad?"

The poor pony was old enough to know
How to hide his pain, to not let it show.
Casper sighed and lay down his head.
In minutes, the old pony was dead.

Shadow made it through the clubbing okay
but the worst was soon to come his way.

He was hung from the ceiling, back legs tied with wire,
His whole body was burning as if it were on fire.
His neck was slashed and he was left there
Left to bleed to death, to die in despair.

"If only I had not lost that race,
Maybe I would not be in this place.
Oh why am I here? What have I done?
Was it something worse than not wanting to run?"

"My blood is spilling on the floor
Oh, please, please I can't take anymore!
I promise I'll try harder if you just let me live
I'll give anything and everything if you just let me live!"

Shadow closed his eyes and breathed out one last sigh
And most painfully the young racer died.
They collected his body along with the others.
Old horses, young horses, the foals with no mothers.

These fifty some horses were butchered for meat
So the disgusting human race would have a delicacy to eat.
The horses did nothing to deserve this fate.
Now they are just meat on a dinner plate.

Reproduced as written by Noelle Snyder, age 12–13

Stages of the Writing Process

Stage 1: Prewriting (Brainstorming)

In a writing workshop format, the teacher needs to first model this stage for the students. With pre-writing, the writer thinks about what he/she already knows about the topic he/she plans to write about and writes down what is known. Writers may **brainstorm** to discover what they already know and what remains to be learned about informational types of topics. **Questions** may be generated and lists made of possible sources of information. The information is then gathered and organized for the next stage. If the writing is narrative, the writer thinks of ideas for characters, setting, problems, events, and other story elements. Students may engage in **free writing** for about ten minutes on an assigned or self-selected topic, about a real or imagined event, in order to have them catch the flow of their thoughts and feelings in a nonstop writing exercise. They may also engage in **rehearsing**, or writing in their heads, composing articles, stories, and other pieces. Later "pen is put to paper" as the student begins to write his/her "rehearsed" piece.

Stage 2: Drafting

Drafting involves actually putting the pencil to paper. This **composing** stage focuses on content, not mechanics. In essence, it is focused only on getting the principal ideas down on paper without worrying about spelling, sentence structure, word choice, punctuation, capitalization, etc. Teachers must reassure students that they will have time later to revise and edit their piece, so it's important to just focus on their content, getting their ideas down on paper during this stage. There may be two or more drafts. The teacher should help writers focus on their audiences by teaching students to ask themselves: "What is my topic?"; "Why am I writing this piece?"; "Who will read my piece?"; "What might they already know about the topic?"; and "What do they need to know?"

Stage 3: Revising

In the revising stage, the writer begins by rereading the draft and making changes on the draft itself. It is important that the teacher model this process so students understand the importance of revision. Some teachers refer to this as the "sloppy copy" stage in that words are often misspelled or crossed out and lines are drawn to indicate where sentences or paragraphs should be moved or inserted. The revision stage often takes place over several days, often involving three or more revisions, depending on the grade level of the writer. The teacher should model how to revise a piece, looking at the **design or format** of a piece, how to **focus a topic**, how to **expand ideas**, and use more **descriptive language**, how to **incorporate dialogue**, etc.

Stage 4: Editing

This stage is the polishing stage. A form of editing takes place in the prewriting stage as the writer thinks about ideas, adopting some and discarding others. A form of editing also takes place in the revising stage as the writer makes decisions about word choice, sentence order, and so on. In the editing stage, the writer reads through the last revised draft, correcting errors in both content and mechanics. The piece of writing is then recopied.

Stage 5: Publishing (Sharing)

In this stage the finished product is shared with the class. This may be done by having each child read his/her final draft from the **Author's Chair**, by making a **class book** of all the students' pieces of writing, by placing all of the final pieces on a **bulletin board**, or by having the writer put his piece in a **book format**. The students should discuss each other's work so that they not only learn from each other but also appreciate each other. An **Authors' Tea** can be conducted once a month or once per grading period to showcase students' writing. Also, teachers can publish students' work by posting it on the class's home-page on the school's website or from http://www.ala.org/greatsites. This web address provides a list of sites that publish children's writing.

A Sample Revision Checklist

_____ Does my piece say what I want it to say?

_____ Will the audience understand it?

_____ Is it interesting?

_____ What might I do to make it more interesting?

_____ Did I give enough details or examples?

_____ Does it sound right?

A Sample Editing Checklist

_____ Is my story clear? Will readers be able to understand it?

_____ Did I write in complete sentences?

_____ Did I capitalize the first word of every sentence?

_____ Did I capitalize the names of people, cities, towns, and other places?

_____ Did I end each sentence with a period, question mark, or exclamation point?

_____ Did I spell all the words correctly?

Checklists reprinted from: Gunning, T. G. (2008). _Creating literacy instruction for all students._ (6th ed.). Boston, MA: Pearson Allyn and Bacon. (pgs. 386, 389)

Writing Workshop Elements (Schedule of a Writing Workshop Session)

1. **Mini-lesson** (5–10 minutes)—presented to the whole class. The purpose is to present a needed writing skill, grammar element, or workshop procedure.

2. **Status of the Class** (2–3 minutes)—presented to the whole class. The purpose is to inform the class what the procedure will be for the day. For example, the teacher will tell which students s/he will be conferencing with that day, which students s/he will work with as a small group for a guided or strategic writing lesson, any information regarding the writing center that may be new, etc.

3. **Guided Writing or Strategic Writing** (10–20 minutes)—presented to a small group of students whose members are at the same stage of writing development. The purpose is to teach a writing strategy, using examples from students' work or selections from children's books. The teacher models the strategy and provides guided practice. Then students apply the skill or strategy in their own writing. The skill or strategy taught should be reviewed, reinforced in conferences, and followed up in lessons until it becomes automatic for these students.

4. **Writing Time** (20–40 minutes, depending on grade level—20 minutes for K–1; 30 minutes for grades 2–3; 40 minutes for grades 4–5)—Students write on self-selected topics. It is very important that writing workshop provides a venue for students to write about their own topics rather than topics assigned by the teacher or writing formats assigned by the teacher. Specific types of writing and topics should be done at other times in the day. It is important during this time that the teacher uses about five minutes to sit down and write (creatively) to demonstrate how s/he works through the writing process. Afterwards, the teacher uses the rest of the writing time to conduct individual conferences with students. On average, a teacher usually can conference with about 5–10 students per day during the writing time of a writer's workshop session.

5. **Group Sharing Time** (10 minutes)—In the last 10 minutes of the writing workshop session, the teacher allows some students who wish to read what they have written so far to the class to receive some feedback from the group. The designated student sits in the Author's Chair and reads his/her piece. The teacher directs some discussion from the class as they provide feedback to the writer.

Sample Writing Conference Monitoring Charts

Name	Date	Topic	Strengths	Needs	Plans
Angelina	11/15	Spending the night with Tamika	Strong beginning	More description of activities that evening	Tell how they baked cookies by themselves
Andy	11/15	Pet parrot	Interesting subject	Not well developed	Give examples of pet's tricks
Carolyn	11/15	Little sister	Good description of sister's traits	More discussion about what she and her sister do together	Develop her topic more and then create a good ending
John		Soccer game			
Robbie		Scary movie			
Stephanie		Dream vacation			
Tamika		New doll			

Example of a Daily Log: Students' Plans for Writing Workshop

Name	Topic	Monday	Tuesday	Wednesday	Thursday	Friday
Angelina	Spending the night with Tamika	D-1, TC	RE			
Andy	Pet parrot	R, TC	PC			
Carolyn	Little sister	R, TC	E			
John	Soccer game	D-1, TC	D-2			
Robbie	Scary movie	E	M			
Stephanie	Dream vacation	P	D-1, TC			
Tamika	New doll	AC	R			

Key:

P: Planning	PE: Peer Editing	PC: Peer Conference
D: Drafting	PUB: Publishing	TC: Teacher Conference
R: Revising	M: Making final copy	AC: Author's circle
E: Editing	RE: Researching	S: Sharing

Adapted from: Muschia, G. R. (1993). Writing workshop survival kit. In T. G. Gunning, *Creating literacy instruction for all students.* (6th ed.). Boston, MA: Pearson Allyn and Bacon.

Helpful Hints for Assisting Writers: What Do You Say When…?

As teachers observe and assist students at various stages of their writing process, they note times when writers seek their support (or the assistance from paraprofessionals, peers, or parent volunteers who may be present during writing workshop sessions). They scaffold instruction when students experience difficulties in spelling or coming up with ideas for writing. It is important that those who assist and support children as they maneuver through the writing process promote independence in solving writing issues. In this way, children will develop as independent writers who are capable of utilizing metacognitive strategies to solve their own problems in developing their written pieces. Below is a list of what teachers may say when students seek assistance during writing workshop.

When the writer says:	You can say:
"I don't know what to write about."	"You have a lot of ideas in your head! Tell me about your favorite…"
	"Tell me about what you did (last night/last weekend/ on vacation)."
	"Tell me about an interesting…"
"I don't know how…"	"Do the best you can…"
"I don't know how to spell…"	"Use your temporary spelling for now."
	"Sound it out and write some clues you hear."
	"Don't worry about correct spelling right now. Just get your ideas down first."
"I don't know how to use temporary spelling…"	"What are you trying to say?"
	"What sounds do you hear?"
When a child shows you his temporary spelling and asks, "What does this say?"	"What do you want it to say?"
"Does this really spell…"	"It's close. Remember the neat thing about temporary spelling is you can spell it how it sounds now, and fix it later!"
"Can you read this?"	"You're giving me a lot of clues (point out a good clue). Would you read it to me?"

Teaching the "Art" of Writing

What are the skills we teach that foster elementary students' writing development? Here are some topics for mini-lessons and/or guided writing, which are small group lessons during the Writing Workshop session.

Expository/Non-Fiction Writing Skills

- Writing clear, complete sentences
- Writing a lead or beginning sentence (often gives main idea of piece and should grab the reader's interest and entice the reader to read it)
- Developing informational pieces with details, including facts, opinions, examples, descriptions (major flaw in students' writing is the failure to develop a topic)
- Writing an effective ending that provides a summary of piece and/or restates main point of piece in a way that impacts the reader
- Using precise, varied, vivid words rather than boring, ordinary words
- Using a thesaurus to help achieve varied vocabulary
- Gathering appropriate and sufficient information for a piece
- Using advanced writing devices (alliteration, rhetorical questions, etc.)
- Using varied sentence patterns
- Combining short sentences into longer ones
- Writing in a variety of expository forms (announcements, newspaper articles, etc.)
- Writing for a variety of purposes and audiences
- Providing transitions so that one thought leads into another smoothly—writing flows logically
- Creating headings and subheadings for longer expository pieces
- Eliminating details that detract from piece

Narrative/Fictional Writing Skills

- Writing a story with strong beginning, middle, and end
- Developing believable characters by using description, action, dialogue
- Creating a setting
- Developing an interesting plot using elements of plot, such as rising action, episodes, problem, resolution, etc.
- Creating interesting endings, including surprise endings
- Writing natural-sounding dialogue
- Creating a title that makes the reader want to read the piece
- Building suspense
- Using advanced fiction techniques (flashback, foreshadowing, in media res, etc.)
- Using figurative language (similes, metaphors, personification, etc.)

Writing Workshop

Types of Conferences

Conferring is a critical component of the writing process approach. During a writing workshop session, a teacher typically holds a variety of conferences with students, depending on each writer's needs. These conferences range from a momentary discussion to a five minute interplay or an extensive exploration of ideas for writing, solving an issue with structure or format, or helping students to be more effective word-smiths. **Five types of writing conferences include:**

- Content conferences
- Design conferences
- Process conferences
- Evaluation conferences
- Editing conferences

Calkins (1994) explains that while writing and conferring, writers *pull in* as they compose. Then they *push back* to consider what they have written so far and **ask questions** to reflect *critically* about the piece:

- What have I said so far? What am I trying to say?
- How do I like it? What is good in my piece that I can build on? What is not so good that I can fix?
- How does it sound? How does it look?
- What else can I say?
- Am I making sense? Will my readers understand what I'm trying to say? What questions will they have? How will they feel? How will they think?
- How else could I approach this?
- What am I learning as I'm writing this?
- What am I going to do next?

Lucy Calkins (1986, 1994) asserts that the first phase of a conference is to do some **research** about the writer in order to understand how the writer engages in the writing process. Not only does the teacher read or listen to the writer's draft, the teacher must be a good listener as the writer talks about her triumphs and difficulties in writing the piece. Then the teacher moves to the **decision** phase of the conference, deciding on a specific focus for the rest of the conference by thinking, *"What does this writer need to hear from me? What can I say to help this writer?"* Here, the teacher determines whether to center the discussion around the subject of the piece, the format the writer has chosen, or the actual process the writer is going through to that point. Now, the teacher moves to the **teaching** phase of the conference in which s/he will ask key questions that will guide the writer in specific ways to help the student navigate the writing experience. From the conference experience, the student should walk away with useful learning that helps with composing the current draft, as well as future pieces of writing.

Calkins (1994) reminds us that "we are teaching the writer and not the writing" (pg. 228). As teachers, we must be careful not to make the child's writing a teacher's product with ideas, sentences, beginnings, and endings added or changed that are the teacher's suggestions. The child's final piece must be completely his or her creation. In addition, the teacher must be careful not to convey that she is the critic of the student's drafts. Instead, the writer is the critic of his or her drafts. Through the conferring process, students themselves are guided in ways that help them become critical readers of their own texts. Teachers support writers' development as they learn to reflect critically about what they write, how they format their writing, and the process they take along the way. Most importantly, writers must learn that they are the owners of their writing, not the teacher. As Calkins (1994) states "Our job in a writing conference is to put ourselves out of a job, to interact with students in such a way that they learn how to interact with their own developing drafts" (pg. 229).

Whether these conferences are conducted by the teacher or the writer's peers, the following steps help students construct meaning and take ownership of their writing process. Teachers understand the importance of following these steps as they seek to empower their students to construct meaningful pieces freely with enjoyment and without fear of the red pen. To accomplish this, the teacher must outline these steps for **teacher-to-student** and **student-to-peer** conferences:

Step 1: The writer reads his/her piece out loud (what s/he has written so far).
Step 2: The listener responds. If the piece is confusing, the listener asks questions and responds.
Step 3: The listener focuses on the area of emphasis for that conference, perhaps asking questions about it. The writer teaches the listener about the subject of the piece.
Step 4: The focus shifts to the text. The listener asks "What will you do next, and how will you do it?"

Content Conferences: Teacher-to-Student; Student-to-Peer Conferences

With **content conferences**, the **focus** is on **what** the **writers are discovering and what they wonder about**, rather than what they already know about the subject. It is important to engage the writer to explore further about the subject. The listener (teacher, peer) may ask:

- What surprises you as you write?
- What new connections do you see in your ideas?
- Where is this leading you?
- What are you learning?

Design Conferences: Teacher-to-Student; Student-to-Peer Conferences

The purpose of a **design conference** is to **balance content with form**. Sometimes a writer may simply be writing three stories in one, or has difficulty focusing. To help writers **focus or narrow their ideas** on their piece, the listener (teacher or peer) may ask:

- What is the one thing you most want to get across?
- You know so much about this topic! Of all that you have to say, what is the most important point?
- What was it about this topic that made you choose to write about it?
- You have told about a great many things. One thing I do after I write a draft is to look over it once and ask myself, "What is the most significant thing to *me*? How can *I* make it significant for *my* readers?"

Sometimes, however, writers may be experiencing difficulty deciding how to organize their writing. Whether or not students tend to lean toward specific formats (or genres) of writing, they must be encouraged to think critically about their design choices based on the nature of the subjects they choose to write about. Additional **design conference questions** are listed below. These may be adapted according to the developmental levels of students:

- How did you decide on this particular format for your piece? What others did you consider? What are you going to do next in terms of the format of this writing?
- Do you want to write a poem? A letter? A short story? A memoir? A picture book? A How-To book? A newspaper article? An informational book? A play? A folktale?
- Do you think the shape and pace of your piece works? Where does it work well? Where does it work less well? What could you do next?
- Are there places where the reader may be misled or confused by your piece?
- What have you left out, skimmed over, or expanded in detail? How else could you have divided up your attention in your piece? Do you think another way would work better?

Process and Evaluation Conferences: Teach the Writer, not the Writing . . .

Similar to athletic coaches, teachers are coaches of writers and their writing. As coaches, teachers study their writers to understand how each writer goes about writing a particular piece, what process the writer takes along the way in order to guide and support the student as s/he develops as a writer. The purpose of a **process conference** is to help the writer focus on *how* s/he approached the act of writing the particular piece. What **steps** did the writer take as s/he **proceeded through the writing**? In fact, writers have the opportunity to teach the teacher about what they do when they write. Process conferences are valuable because they help the writer **reflect** on this very important aspect of the writing process and emphasize that writing itself is more than a means to an end. Process conferences have the potential to **help writers grow** as they examine how they begin to write, problems they encounter along the way, what they do as they revise, pull in, and push back. This leads to an understanding that **the process is just as important as the product**! If teachers watch students as they write and talk to them about the strategies the students use while they write, they can assist them as they become more effective in their use of strategies. Following is a list of **process conference questions** that promote writers' development and their use of effective writing strategies:

- How did you go about writing this? Did you just pick up your pencil and write straight through or did you stop and think, or reread? What made you stop?
- What problems did you run into while you were writing this piece? If I had been watching you, how would I have known you were having problems?
- How did you go about finding a topic? Once you found the topic, did you start writing right away or what did you do?
- How is your process of writing changing?
- I notice you made some cross-outs here. What led you to do that?
- What will you do next? What are your options?

The purpose of an **evaluation conference** is to help the writer **evaluate the products s/he creates** through the writing process. After writing several drafts and revisions, writers will often ask the teacher, "Is this good?" or "Am I done?" The teacher's first question should be, "What do you think?" Writers must learn that their *own* assessment of their *own* writing is very important, and as teachers, we are serious when we ask "What do you think?" (Calkins, 1994). This *reflective,* **evaluation conference** provides an excellent opportunity for the writer to **compare** his or her latest piece of writing with others s/he has produced. The writer may also **discuss** what constitutes, in his or her opinion, a good piece of writing. Below is a list of specific questions that may be asked during an **evaluation conference** to help the writer develop as a reflective, critical reader and writer of his or her own texts.

- How does this piece compare with the other pieces you have written this year? Which is the very best? Next best? What makes this one the best? Could you make it even better if you wanted to? Are there ways?
- Are there places in the piece which you think are especially strong? Where are they? What makes you think these are especially good sections?
- What makes a piece of writing really good?
- Of all the kids in the class, which one writes in a way you especially like? What makes you like his or her writing?
- Of all the authors you read, which one writes in a way you especially like? What makes you like his or her writing?
- What do you think would make your writing even better? What are the strengths of your writing? What are the weaknesses?

Editing Conferences: Teacher-to-Student; Student-to-Peer

The purpose of an **editing conference** is to guide and support writers' understanding and knowledge of language conventions while they develop as writers. During the editing conference, the goal is to look for **grammar, spelling, punctuation, capitalization, word choice, sentence structure, paragraphs, clarity, logic, language, etc.** Children also learn to smooth out their language, order their thoughts, make sure ideas are linked together well, and "listen" to the "poetry of one's sentences" (Calkins, 1994, pg. 301). The teacher begins by celebrating the writer's accomplishment in finishing his piece. Then the teacher looks for patterns in errors, rather than try to deal with each error individually. For example, if the teacher notices that his or her fourth grader used dialogue frequently but did not use quotation marks, the teacher could use this time to focus on the proper use of quotation marks, giving the child the opportunity to fix his or her paper before final submission.

It is important to note, however, that teachers must not demand perfection from children, especially those who have severe problems or English language learners, as they negotiate the writing and editing processes. If teachers expect every word to be spelled correctly, every comma and end punctuation mark to be placed correctly, and every verb to be used correctly, then all their students will write will be safe words and short, safe sentences. They will only use words that they know how to spell. Their writing will be dull and lifeless, because children will be afraid to take risks and explore the language that they hear and speak.

The writer begins by editing his or her piece, using a specific checklist. (See the examples on the following pages). Then s/he gives the completed piece to a peer. It is advantageous for children to edit each other's writing because they learn from one another by sharing strengths, talking about spelling and punctuation, discussing how sentences sound and flow, etc. During the **peer conference**, the peer uses the same checklist to read and edit the piece, write comments, and returns it to the writer. The writer makes additional edits and corrections, if needed. Finally, the writer takes the piece to the **teacher who conducts the final conference** and completes the final edit, including written comments. When the writer brings his self- and peer-edited piece to this final editing conference, and the teacher asks, *"Is this your best?"* The writer should be able to answer emphatically, *"Yes!"* In summary, the editing process is as follows:

Step One: The writer performs a **self-edit** of his or her piece.
Step Two: The writer takes the piece to a peer for **peer editing** conference.
Step Three: The writer has a **teacher-writer editing** conference.
Step Four: The writer performs a final **self-edit, if necessary**.

Adapted from: Calkins, L. M. (1986, 1994). *The art of teaching writing.* Portsmouth, NH: Heinemann.

Expectations for Teaching the Conventions of Writing K-5

	Capitalization	Spelling	Punctuation	Grammar/Usage	Paragraphing/Sentence Fluency
Kindergarten	■ Uses both upper and lower case letters, discerns and discusses the difference ■ Writes first and last name and uses capitals for first letters	■ Awareness of and discusses letter/sound correspondence ■ May begin to spell words phonetically	■ Notices and discusses punctuation marks	■ Awareness of complete sentences in print and speech ■ Uses nouns as labels	■ Awareness of paragraphing ■ Dictates sentences
Grade 1	■ Uses capitals correctly people's names, first word of a sentence, pronoun I ■ Capitalizes days of the week and months of the year	■ Spells grade level, high-frequency words conventionally in final draft; otherwise, spells words phonetically ■ Experiments with expanded vocabulary words	■ Begins to use correct end marks: periods, question marks, and exclamation marks ■ Awareness of use of commas in a series and in appositives; awareness of use of apostrophes in contractions and possessives	■ Identifies simple complete sentences ■ Begins to use sentences with subject-verb agreement ■ Identifies nouns, pronouns, and verbs	■ Recognizes and writes one paragraph ■ Writes a topic sentence with some supporting details ■ Writes a title of a story; includes beginning, middle, and end
Grade 2	■ Capitalizes names of cities, states, holidays, some personal titles, and proper nouns	→	■ Begins to use commas in dates, uses correct end marks: periods, question marks, and exclamation marks	■ Uses complete sentences ■ Varies sentence structure and length ■ Identifies adjectives in sentences ■ Uses nouns, possessive and subject pronouns, and verbs effectively ■ Uses past and present subject/verb agreement	■ Writing simple paragraphs ■ Writes a topic sentence with supporting details ■ Writes a title of a story; includes beginning, middle, and end

Grade					
Grade 3	• Capitalizes holidays, titles, greeting and closing of letters; personal titles, initials, first letter in titles, proper nouns • Awareness of capitalization in dialogue in narrative text	→	• Uses commas for day, month, year; greetings, closing of letters; cities and states • Uses apostrophes correctly in contractions, and possessives • Uses a period at the end of abbreviations • Begins to use quotation marks around spoken words in dialogue	• Writes complete sentences effectively, using nouns, verbs (present and past), adjectives, pronouns, and adverbs • Varies sentence structure and length • Uses homophones correctly (there/their, etc.)	• Begins to use correct paragraphing stanza, divisions, and other textual markers • Can use a main idea sentence effectively • Can compose at least two paragraphs focusing on one topic
Grade 4	• Uses capitalization in dialogue in narrative writing • Uses correct capitalization in titles of books, poems, movies, TV shows, magazines • Uses capitalization correctly in final draft	• Spells grade-level words conventionally in final draft • Spellings on expanded vocabulary words generally conventional	• Consistently uses commas for words in a series; quotation marks and complex sentences • Uses apostrophes correctly in contractions and possessives • Knows and applies the guidelines for simple quotation marks	• Writes a complete sentence using regular and irregular forms of nouns and verbs proficiently • Writes complex sentences • Begins to use the correct verb tense including past, present, and future • Identifies prepositions and prepositional phrases	• Consistently uses correct paragraphing stanza, divisions, and other textual markers • Includes characters, setting, problem, and solution in narrative writing • Uses a main idea sentence effectively; includes strong supporting details • Composes multiple paragraphs focusing on one topic in expository writing • Uses transitional words and phrases for coherency between paragraphs
Grade 5	→	→	• Uses commas correctly in separating clauses and after introductory words • Uses quotation marks correctly in dialogue	• Writes simple, compound, and complex sentences, using various parts of speech, including conjunctions, effectively • Recognizes and begins to use conjunctions and interjections effectively • Uses commas proficiently for comprehensible communication	→ • Uses figurative language in writing

Adapted from: Culham, R. (n.d.). *From NWREL-NWRE: Chart of K-5 Essential Learning and Writing Assessment*. Houghton Mifflin. Retrieved from http://www.sde.idaho.gov/.../NWREL%20Evaluation%20Report%202002....

Chart of Elementary Proofreading Marks

Symbols	Meaning	Example
○	Correct the spelling	I'm a 5-year-old (apaloosa) *appaloosa* mustang mare.
=	Capitalize a letter	I was once wild and lived in South dakota in a mustang sanctuary.
/	Make a capital letter lower case	But Goldilocks has a new little Filly, Whisperer.
^	Insert punctuation	Anyhow‸ I used to teach young children how to (western ride) until a girl was riding me‸ and we were going (to) fast down a hill.
TS	Topic Sentence	
¶	Start a new paragraph	Juliet was furious.¶Anyhow‸ I used to teach young children how to ride western until a girl was riding me‸ and we were going to fast down a hill.
^	Insert a word or words	Then‸ *for* some reason‸ Noelle put Romeo and Black Magic in a pasture with a paint named (Chaparel)
—	Take out or delete	~~Gold Star is grown up now.~~
RO	Run-on Sentence	I tripped‸ ~~and~~ *RO* the girl broke her arm‸ and I broke my leg.
" " ∨ ∨	Insert quotation marks	
~	Reverse letters or words	Anyhow‸ I used to teach young children how to (western ride) until a girl was riding me‸ and we were going (to) fast down a hill.

Sierra Sunshine

I'm Sierra. I'm a 5-year-old (apaloosa) *appaloosa* mustang mare. I was once wild and lived in South dakota in a mustang sanctuary. Then one day‸ some guy came to get me, Black Magic‸ ~~and~~ Romeo, ^*and* 2 other mustangs‸ and we were shipped to Noelle's. The only other horses there were Juliet‸ ~~and~~ Goldilocks‸ and her baby, gold Star. ~~Gold Star is grown up now.~~ But Goldilocks has a new little Filly, Whisperer.¶Anyway, they were nice to us. Romeo fell in love with Juliet, and then he wasn't nervous about our new home. Then, ^*for* some reason‸ Noelle put Romeo and Black Magic in a pasture with a paint named (Chaparel) Juliet was furious.¶Anyhow‸ I used to teach young children how to (western ride) until a girl was riding me‸ and we were going (to) fast down a hill. I tripped‸ ~~and~~ *RO* the girl broke her arm‸ and I broke my leg. Noelle had a vet fix it‸ ~~but~~ he said it would never fully heal, so not even a year ^*after* ~~of~~ being at Noelle's, I was retired. Since I had been through so much, the others named me the lead mare.

Handy Self-Editing Checklist and Rubric—K-2

A Balanced Approach

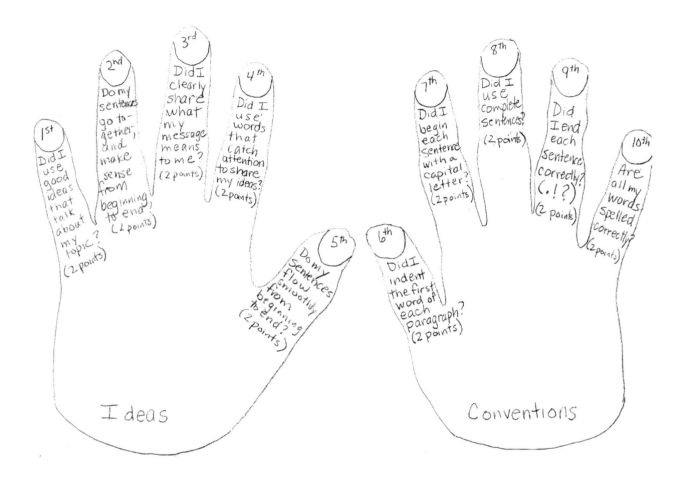

1st Did I use good ideas that talk about my topic? (2 points)

2nd Do my sentences go together, and make sense from beginning to end? (2 points)

3rd Did I clearly share what my message means to me? (2 points)

4th Did I use words that catch attention to share my ideas? (2 points)

5th Do my sentences flow smoothly from beginning to end? (2 points)

6th Did I indent the first word of each paragraph? (2 points)

7th Did I begin each sentence with a capital letter? (2 points)

8th Did I use complete sentences? (2 points)

9th Did I end each sentence correctly? (. ! ?) (2 points)

10th Are all my words spelled correctly? (2 points)

Ideas

Conventions

(Developed by A. F. Snyder and D. J. Coffey)

Editing Checklist (1–3)

Author: _____

Peer Editor: _____

	Self	Peer	Teacher
There is a title.			
Each sentence begins with a capital letter.			
Each sentence ends with a punctuation mark. (. ? !)			
The first sentence is indented.			
Each paragraph is indented.			
Sentence beginnings show variety.			
All words are spelled correctly.			

Peer Comments:

Teacher Comments:

Adapted from: Rasso, A. (1991). Editing checklist. In D. Sumner (Ed.), *A child's window to the world* (pp. 185). Peterborough, NH: The Society for Developmental Education.

Editing Checklist (3–5)

Author: _____

Title: _____

Date Began: _____ Date Finished: _____

Peer Editor: _____

	Self-editor	Peer-editor	Teacher-editor
Does it make sense?	_____	_____	_____
Is all spelling correct?	_____	_____	_____
Is all punctuation correct?	_____	_____	_____

    periods   question marks   commas   exclamation marks   quotation marks

	Self-editor	Peer-editor	Teacher-editor
Are capital letters used correctly? (proper nouns and beginning sentences)	_____	_____	_____
Is paragraphing done correctly? Do paragraphs have topic/main idea sentences?	_____	_____	_____
Are excess words and unnecessary words eliminated?	_____	_____	_____

Peer editor comments:

Teacher comments:

    Strengths—

    Area(s) for Improvement—

Down with Nice

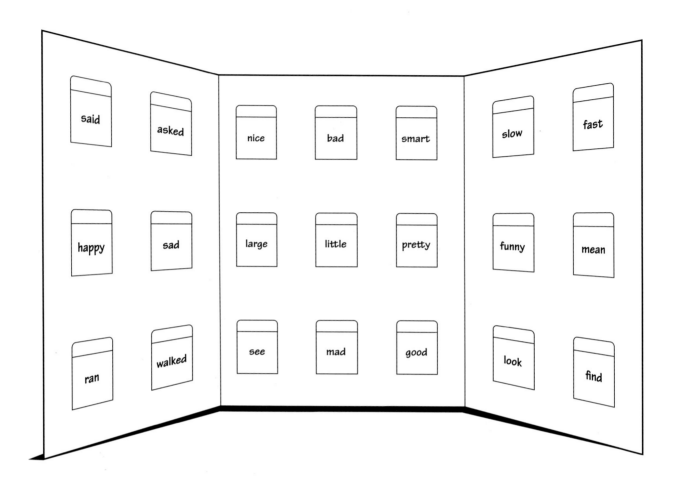

Qualities of Good Writing

Spandel (2005) identified six qualities, or traits, of good writing. These are:

1. **Ideas**—Ideas are the heart of a piece of writing. Students choose an interesting idea, narrow it by focusing on the idea, and develop it using main ideas and details. Choosing an idea takes place during **prewriting** and students develop their ideas as they **draft** and revise their writing.

2. **Organization**—Organization is the framework of the piece. Writers grab the reader's interest in the beginning of their pieces, identify the purpose, present ideas in a logical fashion, provide transitions between ideas, and end with a satisfying conclusion so that the important questions are answered. Writers organize their writing during **prewriting** and follow their plans as they **draft** their pieces.

3. **Voice**—The writer's unique style is voice. Voice is what puts life into a piece of writing. Culham (2003) calls voice "the writer's music coming out through the words" (p. 102). Voice gives the reader a sense that the writer to talking to him or her. During the **drafting** and **revising** stages of writing, the writer creates voice in his piece through the words s/he uses, the sentences the writer creates, and the tone s/he adopts.

4. **Word Choice**—Deliberate, careful word choice makes the meaning clear and the piece more interesting to read. Writers learn to choose active verbs and precise nouns, adjectives, and adverbs. They learn to construct word pictures and use idiomatic expressions as they compose their pieces. They focus on word choice as they **draft** and **revise** their writing.

5. **Sentence Fluency**—Sentence fluency is the rhythm and flow of language. Writers vary the length and structure of their writing so that it has a natural rhythm and is easy to read aloud. They develop sentence fluency as they **draft**, **revise**, and **edit** their writing.

6. **Mechanics/Conventions**—Mechanics/Conventions of writing are spelling, punctuation, capitalization, and grammar. These represent the piece's level of correctness, or how well the writer uses grammar and mechanics with accuracy. In the **editing** stage of the writing process, writers proofread their writing and correct spelling and grammatical errors in order to make their writing easier to read.

Adapted from: Spandel, V. (2005). *Creating writers.* (4th ed.). Portsmouth, NH: Heinemann.
Culham, R. (2003). *6+1 traits of writing: The complete guide grades 3 and up.* New York, NY: Scholastic, Inc.

Publishing—Final Stage of the Writing Process

Materials to Put in Your Writing Center

Book Writing and Illustrating Materials:
- folded white construction paper for interior pages; folded colored construction paper for covers, size 10 × 13
- good pencils, white out, colored pencils, crayons (be sure to have skin tone colors), water paint sets, little plastic cups from Crystal Lite packs, very small-tipped paint brushes, magic markers
- various shape patterns for students to use if they want to make a shape book
- ink pads, various stamps, hand wipes
- a "Down With Nice" tri-fold board
- samples of published picture/chapter books so children can see how title page, copyright page, and author page are written in a children's book

Bookbinding Materials:
- yarn of various colors and large plastic knitting needles for Japanese bookbinding technique
- tag board (cardstock) for book covers or to use for more sturdy under layer of outer cover
- various wallpaper sample sheets to cover the tag board under layer
- brads, metal rings of various sizes
- scissors, glue, rulers, pink pearl erasers, hand held individual hole punchers, double and triple hole punchers

Publishing (Stage 5)
Author's Chair

An Author's Chair:
- gives students a place to share their "work in progress" throughout the writing process and to receive useful feedback from their peers
- gives the writer the opportunity to draw the full attention of his/her peers to a "work in progress" or a "finished piece"
- builds self-confidence and helps students to truly feel like authors and view their writing from an author's perspective
- helps students to be more thoughtful about their audience during the writing process as they give and receive feedback
- gives students a place of distinction to share their "finished work" during the Authors' Tea or other celebrations of writing success

Publishing Stage

Celebrating with an Authors' Tea

An Authors' Tea:
- encourages a love for reading and writing
- enhances acceptance of others
- increases awareness of "presenting" to others
- enriches sight vocabulary
- encourages learning more about a subject
- builds self-confidence
- enriches organizational and planning skills
- models respect and love for literature
- gives *all* children an arena for success
- offers a completed reading and writing cycle that is relevant to children

---

Author's Tea Invitation

_____

Dear _____,

    You are invited to my Author's Tea on _____ at _____. I'll be reading my new book. I need to bring _____ for the party.

           Love,

           _____

Artifact Pondering Sheet

An **Artifact Pondering Sheet** promotes critical thinking in social studies and provides opportunities for students to become intrigued with history as they examine items from the past and present that connect with a topic or theme of study. The teacher gives students a magnifying glass for examining various objects, such as photos, diary pages, tools, documents, maps, utensils, and other objects. As students observe and consider their artifacts, they answer the questions on the pondering sheet. This process gives them insights about the historical context of the artifacts and the geographical and cultural factors that influenced life in that timeframe. Teachers can find artifacts at the local library, museums, garage sales, flea markets, and antique stores.

Artifact Pondering Sheet

As you inspect your artifact, think about and answer the questions below.

1. Examine your artifact. What are some ideas about what it is, and how it might have been used?

2. Who might have used it? Why do you think so?

3. How would you use your background knowledge as you ponder the nature of this artifact?

4. What period of history or particular event does this item bring to mind? Why?

5. Do you think your item has a general geographic home? Might it be more likely to be found in one part of the United States than another? Why?

6. Now read the accompanying picture book. After reading and gathering additional clues from the book, adjust your original speculations about the artifact, if necessary.

7. Explore a relevant website and add several facts to document your speculations or extend your understanding. Use the back of this sheet to write additional information about your artifact. List any books you find as well.

8. Where might you go to gather additional information about the artifact and the topic it represents?

Fuhler, C. J., Farris, P. J., & Nelson, P. A. (2006). Building literacy skills across the curriculum: Forging connections with the past through artifacts. *The Reading Teacher, 59*(7), 646–659.

Double Entry Journals

A **double entry journal** is a reading log that supports students' construction of meaning while reading and taking notes from expository texts. It is a **two-sided** log in which the **left side** is used to write **specific information** about what the author wrote in the text, such as the information listed under *What the Author Said* on the example below. On the **right side** of the page, the student **writes personal responses or reactions** about the information in the text under *What Do You Say? What Are Your Thoughts?* Double entry journals allow readers to engage in a discussion with the author while reflecting about the text in an active, rather than passive manner. Double entry journals are often called dialectic journals and can be used for fiction as well.

Double Entry Journal Framework for Non-Fiction

What the Author Said	What Do You Say? What Are Your Thoughts?
Author's main points/ideas:	Questions you may have about them:
Important details:	Statements that start with *but* or *however:*
Quotable quotes:	Discuss one of the quotes that was meaningful to you. What was your connection with this quote?
	Other knowledge or experience you have on the topic:
Author's conclusions:	Evaluation—reasons you agree or disagree with the author:
Details:	Consequences—results or effects of the author's ideas:

Adapted from: Wood, K. D., & Taylor, D. B. (2006). *Literacy strategies across the subject areas: Process-oriented blackline masters for the K–12 classroom* (2nd ed.). Boston, MA: Pearson Allyn & Bacon.

Other Writing to Learn Activities

Writing to learn activities, such as the ones described below, provide opportunities for students to demonstrate what they have learned from reading in the content areas. It is important to note, however, that these writing activities are not part of the writing process. Students do not rewrite or correct these written products and they are not graded for grammatical errors or mechanics of writing. These activities are designed to promote engagement in the learning process, and the most important aspect is the content of the writing and exploration of concepts.

- **Admit Slips**—Before the class/lesson begins, students write one question or answer one question about the lesson's topic or what was discussed day before. For example, "What is one thing you remember about yesterday's lesson about . . . ?" or "Name and describe one type of simple machine?" Students do not put their names on these slips. Admit slips are placed in a box. The teacher reviews them and uses what s/he learns from them as the motivation or anticipatory set for the new lesson.
- **Exit Slips**—At end of a lesson, students write one question they still have about the lesson's topic, or they write one to three things they learned from the lesson. For example, "What is one thing you learned about . . . ?" or "Write a question you still have about . . . that you still don't understand." Students do not put their names on these slips. Exit slips are placed in a box. The teacher reviews theme and uses what s/he learns from them to plan the next day's lesson.
- **Quickwrites**—These are one-minute writing sessions in which students describe what they know about a given topic or concept. Quickwrites help to activate background knowledge of students, as well as to demonstrate what students have learned during instruction.
- **Found Poems**—Students read a text that goes with a given topic. They pull key phrases that "speak" to them and arrange them into a poem structure without adding any of their own words. This gives students an opportunity to explore the main ideas they have identified about a content area topic from a narrative or expository text. This allows them to transfer the elements of reading to learn to writing to learn, using poetry as the medium.
- **Awards**—Students use knowledge they have gleaned about people of various time frames to write recommendations for awards, such as "Inventor of the Century," "Political Leader of the Century," or "Scientist of the Century."
- **"What if" scenarios**—Students use their knowledge of history or science to predict different possibilities that could have happened in another context. For example, "What if George Washington had been captured by the British?" or "What if the computer was not invented?"
- **Unsent Letters**—Students write letters to various people, past, present, or future. These letters contain specific concepts and ideas from the unit of study or topic of discussion. With unsent letters written to people of the future, students project knowledge of today as they predict events and technological developments of the future that may be factors in the lives of people who will live in years to come.
- **Biopoems**—Students use information gleaned from reading about key people who are integral to the content area being studied. Using the format below, students take the information and write a biography in the form of a poem. (See the next page for an example biopoem sheet.)

Line 1: First name of the biographical person being studied
Line 2: Four adjectives that describe the person
Line 3: Husband/wife/sibling/etc., of . . .
Line 4: Lover of . . . (three things, people, or places)
Line 5: Who feels . . . (three things the person feels)
Line 6: Who fears . . . (three things)
Line 7: Who would like to see . . . (three things)
Line 8: Resident of . . . (city, state, country where the person lived/lives)
Line 9: Last name of the biographical person being studied

- **RAFT (Perspective Writing)**—RAFT stands for Role, Audience, Format, and Topic. RAFT is a technique that provides opportunities for students to write about what they are learning from four different perspectives. When introducing RAFT, everyone writes to the same prompt. Once students have had practice in writing from each perspective, the teacher can assign different components to groups of students, then hold group discussions about a given topic. The four perspectives are listed and described below.

R = role [who is the writer, what is the role of the writer?]
A = audience [to whom are you writing?]
F = format [what format should the writing be in?]
T = topic [what are you writing about?]

Two example RAFT procedures for a writing to learn social studies activity might be:

R	Meriwether Lewis	**R**	William Clark
A	Yankton Sioux Chief	**A**	Thomas Jefferson
F	Directions	**F**	letter
T	How to load a flint lock rifle	**T**	Describing the Pacific Ocean and the geography of the land bordering it

Adapted from: Frey, N., & Fisher, D. (2007). *Reading for information in elementary school: Content literacy strategies to build comprehension.* Upper Saddle River, NJ: Pearson/Merrill Prentice Hall.

Biopoem

_____
[First Name]

Is

_____, _____, _____, _____
[Four adjectives that describe you]

Sibling of

_____
[Sibling (or son, daughter of)]

Lover of

_____, _____, _____
[Three feelings you have and when they are felt]

Who feels

_____, _____, _____
[Three feelings you have and when they are felt]

Who gives

_____, _____, _____
[Three things you give]

Who fears

_____, _____, _____
[Three fears you have]

Who would like to see

_____, _____, _____
[Three things you would like to see]

Who lives

_____
[The town or a brief description of where you live]

_____
Your last name

References

Anders, P., & Bos, C. (1986). Semantic feature analysis: An interactive strategy for vocabulary development and text comprehension. *Journal of Reading, 29*(7), 610–616.

Anderson, R. C., & Pearson, P. D. (1984). A schema-theoretic view of basic processes in reading comprehension. *Handbook of Reading Research.* New York, NY: Longman.

Bear, D., Invernizzi, M., Templeton, S., & Johnson, F. (2000). *Words their way* (2nd ed.). Upper Saddle River, NJ: Prentice Hall.

Beck, I. L., & McKeown, M. G. (2006). *Improving comprehension with questioning the author.* New York, NY: Scholastic.

Beck, I. L., McKeown, M. G., & Kucan, L. (2002). *Bringing words to life: Robust vocabulary instruction.* New York, NY: Guilford.

Beck, I. L., McKeown, M. G., & Omanson, R. C. (1987). The effects and uses of diverse vocabulary instructional techniques. In M. G. McKeown & M. E. Curtis (Eds.), *The nature of vocabulary acquisition* (pp. 147–163). Hillsdale, NJ: Erlbaum.

Beck, I. L., McKeown, M. G., Hamilton, R. L., & Kucan, L. (1997). *Questioning the author: An approach for enhancing student engagement with text.* Newark, DE: International Reading Association.

Bereiter, C., Biemiller, A., Campione, J., Carruthers, I., Fuchs, D., Fuchs, L., et al., (2008). *SRA Imagine it!* Columbus, OH: McGraw Hill.

Blachowicz, C. (1986). Making connections: Alternatives to the vocabulary notebook. *Journal of Reading, 29*(7), 643–649.

Buros, J. (1991). Are you ready for publication? In D. Sumner (Ed.). *A child's window to the world* (pp. 180). Peterborough, NH: The Society for Developmental Education.

Calkins, L. M. (1986/ 1994). *The art of teaching writing.* Portsmouth, NH: Heinemann.

Carr, E., & Ogle, D. M. (1987). K-W-L-Plus: A strategy for comprehension and summarization. *Journal of Reading, 30,* 626–631.

Caverly, D. C., Mandeville, T. F., & Nicholson, S. A. (1995). PLAN: A study-reading strategy for informational text. *Journal of Adolescent and Adult Literacy, 39*(3), 190–199.

Cloonan, K. L. (1991). Author planning page. In D. Sumner (Ed.). *A child's window to the world* (pp. 187). Peterborough, NH: The Society for Developmental Education.

Culham, R. (n. d.). *From NWREL-NWRE: Chart of K-5 Essential Learning and Writing Assessment.* Houghton Mifflin. Retrieved from http://www.sde.idaho.gov/.../NWREL%20Evaluation%20Report%202002...

Culham, R. (2003). *6+1 traits of writing: The complete guide grades 3 and up.* New York, NY: Scholastic, Inc.

Cunningham, J. (1982). Generating interactions between schemata and text. In J. Niles & L. Harris (Eds.), *New inquiries in reading research and instruction, thirty-first yearbook of the National Reading Conference* (pp. 42–47). Washington, DC: National Reading Conference.

Dale, E. (1965). Vocabulary measurement: Techniques and major findings. *Elementary English, 42,* 82–88.

Flint, A. S. (2008). *Literate lives: Teaching reading & writing in elementary classrooms.* Hoboken, NJ: John Wiley & Sons, Inc.

Frayer, D. A., Frederick, W. C., & Klausmeier, H. J. (1969). *A schema for testing the level of concept mastery.* Technical Report No. 16. Madison, WI: University of Wisconsin Research and Development Center for Cognitive Learning.

Frey, N., & Fisher, D. (2007). *Reading for information in elementary school: Content literacy strategies to build comprehension.* Upper Saddle River, NJ: Pearson, Merrill-Prentice Hall.

Fuhler, C. J., Farris, P. J., & Nelson, P. A. (2006). Building literacy skills across the curriculum: Forging connections with the past through artifacts. *The Reading Teacher, 59*(7), 646–659.

Gardner, H. (1983). *Frames of mind.* New York, NY: Basic Book Inc.

Gardner, H. (2006). *Multiple intelligences.* New York, NY: HarperCollins.

Gentry, J. R. & Gillet, J. W. (1993). *Teaching kids to spell.* Portsmouth, NH: Heinemann.

Georgia Department of Education. (2012). *Common Core Georgia Performance Standards: CCGPS. K-12 Educator Resource.* Retrieved from https://www.georgiastandards.org/Common-Core/Documents/CCGPS_ELA_K-12_EducatorResourceDocument.pdf

Graves, D. H. (1983). *Writing: Teachers and children at work.* Portsmouth, NH: Heinemann.

Gunning, T. G. (2000). *Creating literacy for all children* (3rd ed.). Boston, MA: Allyn and Bacon.

Gunning, T. G. (2008). *Creating literacy instruction for all students* (6th ed.). Boston, MA: Pearson Allyn and Bacon.

Haggard, M. R. (1986). The vocabulary self-selection strategy: Using student interest and word knowledge to enhance vocabulary growth. *Journal of Reading, 29* (7), 634–642.

Hansen, J. (2001). *When writers read* (2nd ed.). Portsmouth, NH: Heinemann.

Harvey, S., & Goudvis, A. (2000). *Strategies that work: Teaching comprehension to enhance understanding.* York, ME: Stenhouse.

Herber, H. L. (1978). Teaching reading in content areas (2nd ed.). In K. D. Wood & D. Bruce Taylor (Eds.), *Literacy strategies across the subject areas: Process-oriented blackline masters for the K-12 classroom* (pp. 71–74). Boston, MA: Pearson.

Hoffman, J. V. (1992). Critical reading/thinking across the curriculum: Using I-Charts to support learning. In K. D. Wood & D. Bruce Taylor (Eds.), *Literacy strategies across the subject areas: Blackline masters for the K–12 classroom* (pp.51–53). Boston, MA: Pearson.

Landsdown, S. (1991). Increasing vocabulary knowledge using direct instruction, cooperative grouping, and reading in junior high school. *Illinois Reading Council Journal, 19*(4), 15–21.

Langer, J. A., & Applebee, A. N. (1987). *How writing shapes thinking.* Urbana, IL: National Council of Teachers of English.

Manzo, A. (1969). The ReQuest procedure. *Journal of Reading, 13,* 123–126.

McConnell, S. (1992/1993). Talking drawings: A strategy for assisting learners. *Journal of Reading, 36*(4), 260–269.

Moore, D. W., & Moore, S. A. (1986). Possible sentences. In E. K. Dishner, T. W. Bean, J. E. Readence, and D. W. Moore (Eds.). *Reading in the content areas: Improving classroom instruction.* Dubuque, IA: Kendall/Hunt.

Moore, D. W., Readence, J. E., & Rickelman, R. J. (1989). *Prereading activities for content area reading and learning* (2nd ed.). Newark, DE: IRA

Muschia, G. R. (1993). Writing workshop survival kit. In T. G. Gunning, *Creating literacy instruction for all students* (6th ed.). Boston, MA: Pearson Allyn and Bacon.

Nagy, W. (1988). *Teaching vocabulary to improve reading comprehension.* Newark, DE: International Reading Association.

Norton, T., & Jackson Land, B. L. (2008). *50 literacy strategies for beginning teachers, 1–8* (2nd ed.). Upper Saddle River, NJ: Merrill/Prentice Hall.

Ogle, D. S. (1986). K-W-L group instructional strategy. In A. S. Palincsar, D. S. Ogle, B. F. Jones, & E. G. Carr (Eds.), *Teaching reading as thinking* (Teleconference Resource Guide, pp. 11–17). Alexandria, VA: Association for Supervision and Curriculum Development.

Ornstein, R. (1991). *Evolution of consciousness.* New York, NY: Simon and Schuster.

Palinscar, A., & Brown, A. (1984). Reciprocal teaching of comprehension fostering and comprehension monitoring activities. *Cognition and Instruction, 1*(2), 117–175.

Paris, S. G., Cross, D. R., & Lipson, M. Y. (1984). Informed strategies for learning: A program to improve children's reading awareness and comprehension. *Journal of Educational Psychology, 76,* 1239–1252.

Pauk, W. (1974). *How to study in college.* Boston, MA: Houghton Mifflin.

Raphael, T. E. (1984). Teaching learners about sources of information for answering comprehension questions. *Journal of Reading, 27,* 303–311.

Raphael, T. E. (1986). Teaching Question Answer Relationships, revisited. *Reading Teacher, 39,* 516–522.

Rasso, A. (1991). Editing checklist. In D. Sumner (Ed.), *A child's window to the world* (pp. 185). Peterborough, NH: The Society for Developmental Education.

Richardson, J. S. & Morgan, R. F. (2003). *Reading to learn in the content areas* (5th ed.). Belmont, CA: Thomson Wadsworth Publishing.

Richardson, J. S., Morgan, R. F., & Fleener, C. (2006). *Reading to learn in the content areas* (6th ed.). Belmont, CA: Thomson Wadsworth.

Richek, M. A. (2005). Words are wonderful: Interactive, time-efficient strategies to teach meaning vocabulary, *The Reading Teacher, 58*(5), 414–423.

Rumelhart, D. E. (1980). Schemata: The building blocks of cognition. In R. J. Spiro, B. C. Bruce, & W. F. Brewer (Eds.), *Theoretical issues in reading comprehension.* Hillsdale, NJ: Erlbaum.

Schwartz, R. (1988). Learning to learn vocabulary in content area textbooks. *Journal of Reading, 32,* 108–118.

Snyder, A. F. (2003). *An examination of reading interactions between mothers and their daughters in grades four through six.* Unpublished doctoral dissertation, University of Pittsburgh, Pittsburgh, PA.

Snyder, A. F. (2009). *Research-based strategies for literacy instruction in grades 3–5.* Dubuque, IA: Kendall-Hunt.

Spandel, V. (2005). *Creating writers* (4th ed.). Portsmouth, NH: Heinemann.

Stauffer, R. G. (1969). *Directing reading maturity as a cognitive process.* New York, NY: Harper Row.

Tierney, R. J., & Readence, J. E. (2000). *Reading strategies and practices: A compendium* (5th ed.). Boston, MA: Allyn & Bacon.

Tompkins, G. E. (2003). *Literacy for the 21st century* (3rd ed.). Upper Saddle River, NJ: Merrill Prentice-Hall.

Vacca, R. T. & Vacca, J. L. (1996). *Content area reading* (5th ed.). New York, NY: HarperCollins.

Viola, H. (2005). *Social studies. United States history: Early years.* Boston, MA: Houghton Mifflin.

Wiener, H. S., & Bazerman, C. (1994). *Reading skills handbook* (6th ed.). Boston, MA: Houghton Mifflin.

Wood. K. D. (1988). Guiding students through informational text. *The Reading Teacher, 41*(9), 912–920.

Wood, K. D., Lapp, D., & Flood, J. (1992). *Guiding readers through text: A review of study guides.* Newark, DE: International Reading Association.

Wood, K. D., Lapp, D., Flood, J., & Taylor, D. B. (2008). *Guiding readers through text: Strategy guides for new times.* Newark, DE: International Reading Association.

Wood, K. D., & Taylor, D. B. (2006). *Literacy strategies across the subject areas: Process-oriented blackline masters for the K-12 classroom* (2nd ed.). Boston, MA: Pearson/Allyn & Bacon.

Children's Book References

Ammon, R. (2000). *Conestoga wagons*. New York, NY: Holiday House.

Briggs Martin, J. (2009). *Snowflake Bentley*. New York, NY: Houghton Mifflin Publishers.

Bunting, E. (1995). *Dandelions*. Orlando, FL: Sandpiper Books/Harcourt Publishers.

Burchard, P. (1999). *Lincoln and slavery*. New York, NY: Atheneum Books for Young Readers.

Gallaz, C. (1985). *Rose Blanche*. Mankato, MA: Creative Paperbacks, Inc.

Golenbock, P. (1992). *Teammates*. Orlando, FL: Voyager Books/Harcourt Publishers.

Hatkoff, I., Hatkoff, C., & Kahumbu, P. (2006). *Owen and Mzee: The true story of a remarkable friendship*. New York, NY: Scholastic.

Hazen, B. S. (1983). *Tight times*. New York, NY: Puffin Books.

Jeunesse, G., Delafosse, C., Fuhr, U., & Sautai, R. (1993). *Whales*. New York, NY: Scholastic.

Pellant, C. (2000). *The best book of fossils, rocks, and minerals*. New York, NY: Kingfisher Publications.

Steig, W. (1971). *Amos & Boris*. New York, NY: Farrar, Straus, and Giroux Publishers.

World Wildlife Fund. (1988). *All about tigers*. Washington, DC: Author.

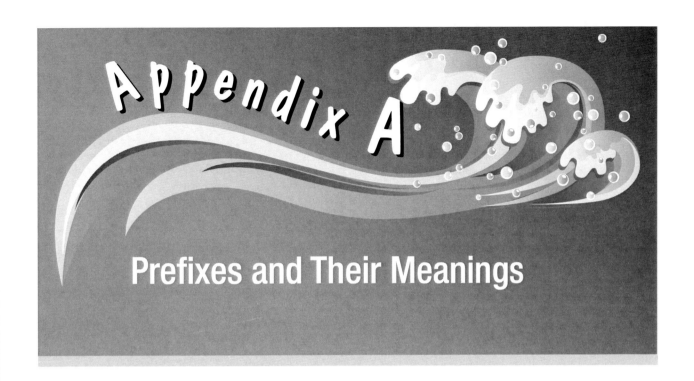

Prefixes and Their Meanings

A **prefix** is a morpheme that comes at the beginning of a root word or base word. A prefix carries meaning.

Prefix	Meaning	Sample Word(s)
1. a, an	without	anaerobic
2. ab	Away, from	abnormal
3. ad	to, toward	adhere
4. aero	air	aerobic
5. ambi, amphi	both	ambidextrous
6. ante	before	antebellum
7. anti	against, opposite	antibiotic
8. auto	self	autobiography, automobile
9. bene, bon	good	beneficiary, benefactor
10. bi	two	biped
11. bio	life	biology, biography
12. circum	around	circumnavigate
13. com, con, co	together, with	combine, co-exist, commune
14. chrono	time	chronology
15. contra, contro	against	contradict
16. di, dis	two	dissect
17. de	out of, reverse, away	deport, desegregate
18. deci	ten	decibels, decimal
19. demi	half	demitasse

Prefix	Meaning	Sample Word(s)
20. dis	not	dislike, distrust
21. dia	through, across	dialect, diameter
22. dys	abnormal, bad	disfunctional, dystrophy
23. ex, e	out, from, out of, prior to	excrete, exit, expel
24. extra, extro	outside, beyond	extraterrestrial
25. geo	earth	geology
26. gen	race, kind	generation
27. hyper	over, excess	hyperactive
28. hypo	under, less	hypoactive
29. homo	same, alike	homogeneous
30. hetero	mixed	heterogeneous
31. hemi	half	hemisphere
32. in	not	inactive, incapable
33. in, en	into	inbreed, endure
34. inter	between	interstate, interact
35. intra	within	intrastate
36. iso	equal	isometric
37. macro	large	macroscopic
38. micro	small	microscopic, microbe
39. mega	huge	megaphone, megabucks
40. magni	great, large	magnify
41. meta	change, beyond	metamorphosis
42. mono	one	monogram, monologue
43. mis	bad, badly, wrong, wrongly	misdiagnose, mislead
44. multi	many	multilingual
45. neo	new, recent	neonatal
46. non	not	nonalchoholic, nonabrasive
47. octo	eight	octopus, octagon
48. omni	all	omnipresent, omniferous
49. ortho	straight	orthotics, orthodontics
50. osteo	bone	osteoporosis
51. over	above, beyond	overdue, overflow
52. pedi, pod	foot, footed	podiatrist, pedal
53. pan	all	panorama, pandemic
54. para	beside, near, beyond	paranormal, paralegal

Prefix	Meaning	Sample Word(s)
55. per	through	permeate
56. phono	sound, voice	phonograph
57. photo	light	photograph
58. poly	many, much	polygon, polygamist
59. pos, pon	place, put	position
60. post	after	postnatal, postdate
61. pre	before	preview, predate, prehistoric
62. pro	for, forward	procreate, proactive
63. pseudo	false	pseudonym
64. psycho	mind	psychology
65. quad	four	quadrilateral
66. retro	backward	retroactive, retrospective
67. semi	half	semicircle
68. sub	under	submarine, subversive
69. syn, sym	together, with	synthesis, symphony
70. super	over, above, beyond	superimpose, supervise
71. tele	far, distant	telescope, telephone
72. ten	to hold	tenacious, tentacles
73. thermo	heat	thermometer
74. trans	across	transcontinental, transient
75. un	not	undeveloped, undo
76. under	below	understate, underwear
77. uni	one	unicycle
78. vita	life	vitality, vitamin
79. zoo	animal	zoology
80. be	make	belittle

Suffixes and Their Meanings

A **suffix** is a morpheme that is placed at the end of a root word or base word. A suffix carries meaning.

Suffix	Meaning	Example Words
1. able, ible	capable of	intangible-not capable of being touched or reached plausible-capable of being trusted reprehensible-blamable
2. ac, ic	like, pertaining to	eclectic-choosing ideas, methods from various sources dogmatic-opinionated; having opinions without proof lethargic-like having a lack of energy
3. ant	one who	assistant- one who assists
4. ar	one who	liar-one who lies
5. arium	place for	aquarium-a place for fish or other water life
6. tude	state of	certitude-state of being sure, certain gratitude-state of being thankful, gracious
7. ary	like, connected with	adversary-opponent; one who opposes or resists arbitrary-proceeding from a whim or fancy
8. ation	the act of	imputation-the act of accusation approbation-the act of praising, commending adulation-flattering and giving excessive praise
9. ous	full of	ludicrous- absurd; ridiculous facetious-full of joking malodorous-full of unpleasant odor
10. eer, er, or	person who	conductor- a person who leads, conducts, manages censor- a person who finds faults; an adverse critic slanderer-a person who gives false information about another person which is damaging in nature

Continued.

Suffix	Meaning	Example Words
11. ent	one who	resident-one who resides or lives
12. ling	small	fledgling- a small bird or baby chicken
13. escent	becoming	obsolescent-becoming obsolete; going out of use or style iridescent-becoming colorful like the rainbow
14. fic	making, doing	horrific-to make horrifying omnific-all-creating
15. fy	to make	rectify-to make better a situation that was created by the person who caused the problem vivify-to make vivid; to enliven
16. iferous	producing, bearing	vociferous-producing loud, noisy outcries to make one's own feelings known coniferous-bearing or producing cones
17. il, ile	capable of	puerile-childish; silly; immature docile-easy to manage or discipline
18. ism	doctrine, belief	monotheism-belief that there is only one God misoneism-hatred of anything new
19. ist	dealer, doer	anarchist-someone who believes in and promotes anarchy or lack of rule or government antagonist-someone who opposes or competes with another; opponent
20. ity	state of being	fidelity-state of being faithful
21. ive	like	pensive-thoughtful in a sad way; melancholy apprehensive-fearful of what may come
22. oid	resembling	crystalloid-resembling crystal anthropoid-resembling man; manlike
23. osis	condition	neurosis-psychic or mental disorder of such conditions as phobias, depression, anxiety symbiosis-two unlike organisms living together in mutually helpful association
24. y	state of	sunny-state of having lots of sunshine
25. ology	study of	mythology-the study of mythical stories anthropology-the study of man
26. ness	state of being	happiness-state of being happy
27. less	without	penniless-without money
28. ery, ry	products	pottery-products made from clay
29. ful	full of	mouthful-mouth is full of
30. ess	one who (female)	actress-woman who acts
31. ish	of or belonging to a nationality; like or characteristic of; verging on; somewhat, rather; about; ending on some verbs from French verb origins	spanish; boyish; bookish; tallish, bluish; thirtyish; finish (finir), punish (punir)
32. ment	a result or product; a means; the act, fact; the state, condition	compartment; excitement; amusement; appointment;

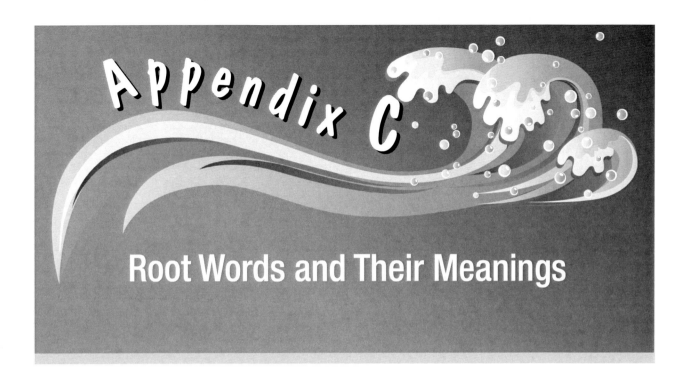

Root Words and Their Meanings

Root words are morphemes that cannot stand alone. They need additional word parts added to them in order to form a complete word in English. Roots have origins in various languages, such as French, Latin, Greek, Old English, etc.

Root	Meaning	Sample Word
1. ac	sharp	acupuncture
2. agog	leader	pedagogue
3. agri	field	agriculture
4. ali	another	alimony
5. alter	other	altercation
6. am	love	amity, amnesty
7. anim	mind, soul	animosity, anisism
8. ann, enn	year	annual, perennial
9. anthrop	man	anthropology
10. aqua, aque	water	aqueduct
11. arch	ruler, first	archbishop
12. aster	star	asteroid
13. aud	hear	auditory
14. auto	self	autonomous
15. belli	war	belligerent
16. ben	good	benevolent
17. biblio	book	bibliography

Continued.

Root	Meaning	Sample Word
18. bio	life	biology, autobiography
19. breve	short	brevity, abbreviate
20. cap	to take	capture, captivate
21. cess	to yield, to go	incessant
22. cent	one hundred	centenary, century
23. chron	time	chronological, synchronize
24. cid, cis	to cut, to kill	fratricide, homicide, scissors
25. cit	to call, to start	citation, incite
26. clam	to cry out	exclamatory, exclaim
27. cognit	to learn	cognition, recognize
28. corpor	body	corporation, corporal
29. da, dat	to give	data
30. dic, dict	to say	dictation, diction
31. doc, doct	to teach	doctrine, indoctrinate
32. dynamo	power, strength	dynamic, dynamite
33. err	to wander	erroneous, erratic
34. fall, fals	to deceive	falsify
35. fid	belief, faith	fidelity, confidence
36. frag, fract	to break	fracture, fragment
37. gam	marriage	monogamy, polygamy
38. grad	go, step	gradual, graduate, gradation
39. gram	writing	telegram, monogram
40. gress	go, step	transgress, Congress, progression
41. it	journey	itinerant, itinerary
42. liber	book	library, librarian
43. logu	to talk	dialogue, monologue
44. luc	light	lucent, luciferous, translucent
45. magn	great	magnify, magnificent, magnanimous
46. man	hand	emancipate
47. mon, monit	to warn	premonition, monitor
48. morph	shape, form	morphology, metamorphosis
49. nat	born	prenatal, nativity
50. nov	new	novice, novelty
51. omni	all	omniferous
52. pac	peace	pacify

Root	Meaning	Sample Word
53. pater, part	father	paternity, patriarch
54. ped, pud	foot	pedestrian, pedal
55. phil	love	philanthropist, philosophy
56. psych	mind	psychiatrist, psychology
57. ques, quir	to ask	question, queries, inquiry
58. rid, ris	laugh	ridiculous, ridicule
59. rupt	to break, lender	disruption, corrupt
60. sci	to know	science
61. sect	to cut	section, dissect
62. sequi, secut	to follow	sequel, sequence
63. tempro	time	temporary, temporal
64. therm	heat	thermos, thermometer
65. urb	city	suburb, urban
66. vac	empty	vacuum, evacuate, vacant
67. vid, vis	to see	evident, visible
68. viv, vit	alive	vivify, vivacious
69. vol	wish	volition, voluntary
70. volv, volut	to roll	revolution, evolve

Common Core Standards for Writing K–5

Writing Standards K–5

The following standards for K–5 offers a focus for instruction each year to help ensure that students gain adequate mastery of a range of skills and applications. Each year in their writing, students should demonstrate increasing sophistication in all aspects of language use, from vocabulary and syntax to the development and organization of ideas, and they should address increasingly demanding content and sources. *Students advancing through the grades are expected to meet each year's grade-specific standards and retain or further develop skills and understandings mastered in preceding grades.*

Kindergartners:	Grade 1 students:	Grade 2 students:
Text Types and Purposes		
1. Use a combination of drawing, dictating, and writing to compose opinion pieces in which they tell a reader the topic or the name of the book they are writing about and state an opinion or preference about the topic or book (e.g., *My favorite book is . . .*).	1. Write opinion pieces in which they introduce the topic or name the book they are writing about, state an opinion, supply a reason for the opinion, and provide some sense of closure.	1. Write opinion pieces in which they introduce the topic or book they are writing about, state an opinion, supply reasons that support the opinion, use linking words (e.g., *because, and, also*) to connect opinion and reasons, and provide a concluding statement or section.
2. Use a combination of drawing, dictating, and writing to compose informative/explanatory texts in which they name what they are writing about and supply some information about the topic.	2. Write informative/explanatory texts in which they name a topic, supply some facts about the topic, and provide some sense of closure.	2. Write informative/explanatory texts in which they introduce a topic, use facts and definitions to develop points, and provide a concluding statement or section.

Continued.

Kindergartners:	Grade 1 students:	Grade 2 students:
Text Types and Purposes—cont'd		
3. Use a combination of drawing, dictating, and writing to narrate a single event or several loosely linked events, tell about the events in the order in which they occurred, and provide a reaction to what happened.	3. Write narratives in which they recount two or more appropriately sequenced events, include some details regarding what happened, use temporal words to signal event order, and provide some sense of closure.	3. Write narratives in which they recount a well-elaborated event or short sequence of events, include details to describe actions, thoughts, and feelings, use temporal words to signal event order, and provide a sense of closure.
Production and Distribution of Writing		
4. (Begins in grade 3)	4. (Begins in grade 3)	4. (Begins in grade 3)
5. With guidance and support from adults, respond to questions and suggestions from peers and add details to strengthen writing as needed.	5. With guidance and support from adults, focus on a topic, respond to questions and suggestions from peers, and add details to strengthen writing as needed.	5. With guidance and support from adults and peers, focus on a topic and strengthen writing as needed by revising and editing.
6. With guidance and support from adults, explore a variety of digital tools to produce and publish writing, including in collaboration with peers.	6. With guidance and support from adults, use a variety of digital tools to produce and publish writing, including in collaboration with peers.	6. With guidance and support from adults, use a variety of digital tools to produce and publish writing, including in collaboration with peers.
Research to Build and Present Knowledge		
7. Participate in shared research and writing projects (e.g., explore a number of books by a favorite author and express opinions about them).	7. Participate in shared research and writing projects (e.g., explore a number of "how-to" books on a given topic and use them to write a sequence of instructions).	7. Participate in shared research and writing projects (e.g., read a number of books on a single topic to produce a report; record science observations).
8. With guidance and support from adults, recall information from experiences or gather information from provided sources to answer a question.	8. With guidance and support from adults, recall information from experiences or gather information from provided sources to answer a question.	8. Recall information from experiences or gather information from provided sources to answer a question.
9. (Begins in grade 4)	9. (Begins in grade 4)	9. (Begins in grade 4)
Range of Writing		
10. (Begins in grade 3)	10. (Begins in grade 3)	10. (Begins in grade 3)

Grade 3 students:	Grade 4 students:	Grade 5 students:
Text Types and Purposes		

1. Write opinion pieces on topics or texts, supporting a point of view with reasons.
  a. Introduce the topic or text they are writing about, state an opinion, and create an organizational structure that lists reasons.
  b. Provide reasons that support the opinion.
  c. Use linking words and phrases (e.g., *because, therefore, since, for example*) to connect opinion and reasons.
  d. Provide a concluding statement or section.
	1. Write opinion pieces on topics or texts, supporting a point of view with reasons and information.
	  a. Introduce a topic or text clearly, state an opinion, and create an organizational structure in which related ideas are grouped to support the writer's purpose.
	  b. Provide reasons that are supported by facts and details.
	  c. Link opinion and reasons using words and phrases (e.g., *for instance, in order to, in addition*).
	  d. Provide a concluding statement or section related to the opinion presented.
		1. Write opinion pieces on topics or texts, supporting a point of view with reasons and information.
		  a. Introduce a topic or text clearly, state an opinion, and create an organizational structure in which ideas are logically grouped to support the writer's purpose.
		  b. Provide logically ordered reasons that are supported by facts and details.
		  c. Link opinion and reasons using words, phrases, and clauses (e.g., *consequently, specifically*).
		  d. Provide a concluding statement or section related to the opinion presented.

2. Write informative/explanatory texts to examine a topic and convey ideas and information clearly.
  a. Introduce a topic and group related information together; include illustrations when useful to aiding comprehension.
  b. Develop the topic with facts, definitions, and details.
  c. Use linking words and phrases (e.g., *also, another, and, more, but*) to connect ideas within categories of information.
  d. Provide a concluding statement or section.
	2. Write informative/explanatory texts to examine a topic and convey ideas and information clearly.
	  a. Introduce a topic clearly and group related information in paragraphs and sections; include formatting (e.g., headings), illustrations, and multimedia when useful to aiding comprehension.
	  b. Develop the topic with facts, definitions, concrete details, quotations, or other information and examples related to the topic.
	  c. Link ideas within categories of information using words and phrases (e.g., *another, for example, also, because*).
	  d. Use precise language and domain-specific vocabulary to inform about or explain the topic.
	  e. Provide a concluding statement or section related to the information or explanation presented.
		2. Write informative/explanatory texts to examine a topic and convey ideas and information clearly.
		  a. Introduce a topic clearly, provide a general observation and focus, and group related information logically; include formatting (e.g., headings), illustrations, and multimedia when useful to aiding comprehension.
		  b. Develop the topic with facts, definitions, concrete details, quotations, or other information and examples related to the topic.
		  c. Link ideas within and across categories of information using words, phrases, and clauses (e.g., *in contrast, especially*).
		  d. Use precise language and domain-specific vocabulary to inform about or explain the topic.
		  e. Provide a concluding statement or section related to the information or explanation presented.

Continued.

Grade 3 students:	Grade 4 students:	Grade 5 students:
Text Types and Purposes—cont'd		

3. Write narratives to develop real or imagined experiences or events using effective technique, descriptive details, and clear event sequences.
  a. Establish a situation and introduce a narrator and/or characters; organize an event sequence that unfolds naturally.
  b. Use dialogue and descriptions of actions, thoughts, and feelings to develop experiences and events or show the response of characters to situations.
  c. Use temporal words and phrases to signal event order.
  d. Provide a sense of closure.
	3. Write narratives to develop real or imagined experiences or events using effective technique, descriptive details, and clear event sequences.
	  a. Orient the reader by establishing a situation and introducing a narrator and/or characters; organize an event sequence that unfolds naturally.
	  b. Use dialogue and description to develop experiences and events or show the responses of characters to situations.
	  c. Use a variety of transitional words and phrases to manage the sequence of events.
	  d. Use concrete words and phrases and sensory details to convey experiences and events precisely.
	  e. Provide a conclusion that follows from the narrated experiences or events.
		3. Write narratives to develop real or imagined experiences or events using effective technique, descriptive details, and clear event sequences.
		  a. Orient the reader by establishing a situation and introducing a narrator and/or characters; organize an event sequence that unfolds naturally.
		  b. Use narrative techniques, such as dialogue, description, and pacing, to develop experiences and events or show the responses of characters to situations.
		  c. Use a variety of transitional words, phrases, and clauses to manage the sequence of events.
		  d. Use concrete words and phrases and sensory details to convey experiences and events precisely.
		  e. Provide a conclusion that follows from the narrated experiences or events.

Production and Distribution of Writing		
4. With guidance and support from adults, produce writing in which the development and organization are appropriate to task and purpose. (Grade-specific expectations for writing types are defined in standards 1–3 above.)	4. Produce clear and coherent writing in which the development and organization are appropriate to task, purpose, and audience. (Grade-specific expectations for writing types are defined in standards 1–3 above.)	4. Produce clear and coherent writing in which the development and organization are appropriate to task, purpose, and audience. (Grade-specific expectations for writing types are defined in standards 1–3 above.)
5. With guidance and support from peers and adults, develop and strengthen writing as needed by planning, revising, and editing. (Editing for conventions should demonstrate command of Language standards 1–3 up to and including grade 3 on pages 28 and 29.)	5. With guidance and support from peers and adults, develop and strengthen writing as needed by planning, revising, and editing. (Editing for conventions should demonstrate command of Language standards 1–3 up to and including grade 4 on pages 28 and 29.)	5. With guidance and support from peers and adults, develop and strengthen writing as needed by planning, revising, and editing, rewriting, or trying a new approach. (Editing for conventions should demonstrate command of Language standards 1–3 up to and including grade 5 on pages 28 and 29.)

Grade 3 students:	Grade 4 students:	Grade 5 students:
6. With guidance and support from adults, use technology to produce and publish writing (using keyboarding skills) as well as to interact and collaborate with others.	6. With some guidance and support from adults, use technology, including the Internet, to produce and publish writing as well as to interact and collaborate with others; demonstrate sufficient command of keyboarding skills to type a minimum of one page in a single sitting.	6. With some guidance and support from adults, use technology, including the Internet, to produce and publish writing as well as to interact and collaborate with others; demonstrate sufficient command of keyboarding skills to type a minimum of two pages in a single sitting.

Research to Build and Present Knowledge

Grade 3 students:	Grade 4 students:	Grade 5 students:
7. Conduct short research projects that build knowledge about a topic.	7. Conduct short research projects that build knowledge through investigation of different aspects of a topic.	7. Conduct short research projects that use several sources to build knowledge through investigation of different aspects of a topic.
8. Recall information from experiences or gather information from print and digital sources; take brief notes on sources and sort evidence into provided categories.	8. Recall relevant information from experiences or gather relevant information from print and digital sources; take notes and categorize information, and provide a list of sources.	8. Recall relevant information from experiences or gather relevant information from print and digital sources; summarize or paraphrase information in notes and finished work, and provide a list of sources.
9. (Begins in grade 4)	9. Draw evidence from literary or informational texts to support analysis, reflection, and research. a. Apply *grade 4 Reading standards* to literature (e.g., "Describe in depth a character, setting, or event in a story or drama, drawing on specific details in the text [e.g., a character's thoughts, words, or actions]."). b. Apply *grade 4 Reading standards* to informational texts (e.g., "Explain how an author uses reasons and evidence to support particular points in a text").	9. Draw evidence from literary or informational texts to support analysis, reflection, and research. a. Apply *grade 5 Reading standards* to literature (e.g., "Compare and contrast two or more characters, settings, or events in a story or a drama, drawing on specific details in the text [e.g., how character's interact]"). b. Apply *grade 5 Reading standards* to informational texts (e.g., "Explain how an author uses reasons and evidence to support particular points in a text, identifying which reasons and evidence support which point[s]").

Range of Writing

Grade 3 students:	Grade 4 students:	Grade 5 students:
10. Write routinely over extended time frames (time for research, reflection, and revision) and shorter time frames (a single sitting or a day or two) for a range of discipline-specific tasks, purposes, and audiences.	10. Write routinely over extended time frames (time for research, reflection, and revision) and shorter time frames (a single sitting or a day or two) for a range of discipline-specific tasks, purposes, and audiences.	10. Write routinely over extended time frames (time for research, reflection, and revision) and shorter time frames (a single sitting or a day or two) for a range of discipline-specific tasks, purposes, and audiences.

Language Standards K-5

The following standards for grades K–5 offer a focus for instruction each year to help ensure that students gain adequate mastery of a range of skills and applications. *Students advancing through the grades are expected to meet each year's grade-specific standards and retain or further develop skills and understandings mastered in preceding grades.* Beginning in grade 3, skills and understandings that are particularly likely to require continued attention in higher grades as they are applied to increasingly sophisticated writing and speaking are marked with an asterisk (*).

Kindergartners:	Grade 1 students:	Grade 2 students:
Conventions of Standard English		
1. Demonstrate command of the conventions of standard English grammar and usage when writing or speaking. a. Print many upper- and lowercase letters. b. Use frequently occurring nouns and verbs. c. Form regular plural nouns orally by adding /s/ or /es/ (e.g., *dog, dogs; wish, wishes*). d. Understand and use question words (interrogatives) (e.g., *who, what, where, when, why, how*). e. Use the most frequently occurring prepositions (e.g., *to, from, in, out, on, off, for, of, by, with*). f. Produce and expand complete sentences in shared language activities.	1. Demonstrate command of the conventions of standard English grammar and usage when writing or speaking. a. Print all upper- and lowercase letters. b. Use common, proper, and possessive nouns. c. Use singular and plural nouns with matching verbs in basic sentences (e.g., *He hops, We hop*). d. Use personal, possessive, and indefinite pronouns (e.g., *I, me, my; they, them, their; anyone, everything*). e. Use verbs to convey a sense of past, present, and future (e.g., *Yesterday I walked home; Today I walk home; Tomorrow I will walk home*). f. Use frequently occurring adjectives. g. Use frequently occurring conjunctions (e.g., *and, but, or, so, because*). h. Use determiners (e.g., articles, demonstratives). i. Use frequently occurring prepositions (e.g., *during, beyond, toward*). j. Produce and expand complete simple and compound declarative, interrogative, imperative, and exclamatory sentences in response to prompts.	1. Demonstrate command of the conventions of standard English grammar and usage when writing or speaking. a. Use collective nouns (e.g., *group*). b. Form and use frequently occurring irregular plural nouns (e.g., *feet, children, teeth, mice, fish*). c. Use reflexive pronouns (e.g., *myself, ourselves*). d. Form and use the past tense of frequently occurring irregular verbs (e.g., *sat, hid, told*). e. Use adjectives and adverbs, and choose between them depending on what is to be modified. f. Produce, expand, and rearrange complete simple and compound sentences (e.g., *The boy watched the movie. The little boy watched the movie; The action movie was watched by the little boy*).

Kindergartners:	Grade 1 students:	Grade 2 students:
Conventions of Standard English—cont'd		
2. Demonstrate command of the conventions of standard English capitalization, punctuation, and spelling when writing. a. Capitalize the first word in a sentence and the pronoun *I*. b. Recognize and name end punctuation. c. Write a letter or letters for most consonant and short-vowel sounds (phonemes). d. Spell simple words phonetically, drawing on knowledge of sound-letter relationships.	2. Demonstrate command of the conventions of standard English capitalization, punctuation, and spelling when writing. a. Capitalize dates and names of people. b. Use end punctuation for sentences. c. Use commas in dates and to separate single words in a series. d. Use conventional spelling for words with common spelling patterns and for frequently occurring irregular words. e. Spell untaught words phonetically, drawing on phonemic awareness and spelling conventions.	2. Demonstrate command of the conventions of standard English capitalization, punctuation, and spelling when writing. a. Capitalize holidays, product names, and geographic names. b. Use commas in greetings and closings of letters. c. Use an apostrophe to form contractions and frequently occurring possessives. d. Generalize learned spelling patterns when writing words (e.g., cage → badge; boy → boil). e. Consult reference materials, including beginning dictionaries, as needed to check and correct spellings.
Knowledge of Language		
3. (Begins in grade 2)	3. (Begins in grade 2)	3. Use knowledge of language and its conventions when writing, speaking, reading, or listening. a. Compare formal and informal uses of English.
Vocabulary Acquisition and Use		
4. Determine or clarify the meaning of unknown and multiple-meaning words and phrases based on *kindergarten reading and content*. a. Identify new meanings for familiar words and apply them accurately (e.g., knowing *duck* is a bird and learning the verb *to duck*). b. Use the most frequently occurring inflections and affixes (e.g., *-ed, -s, re-, un-, pre-, -ful, -less*) as a clue to the meaning of an unknown word.	4. Determine or clarify the meaning of unknown and multiple-meaning words and phrases based on *grade 1 reading and content*, choosing flexibly from an array of strategies. a. Use sentence-level context as a clue to the meaning of a word or phrase. b. Use frequently occurring affixes as a clue to the meaning of a word. c. Identify frequently occurring root words (e.g., *look*) and their inflectional forms (e.g., *looks, looked, looking*).	4. Determine or clarify the meaning of unknown and multiple-meaning words and phrases based on *grade 2 reading and content*, choosing flexibly from an array of strategies. a. Use sentence-level context as a clue to the meaning of a word or phrase. b. Determine the meaning of the new word formed when a known prefix is added to a known word (e.g., *happy/unhappy, tell/retell*). c. Use a known root word as a clue to the meaning of an unknown word with the same root (e.g., *addition, additional*). d. Use knowledge of the meaning of individual words to predict the meaning of compound words (e.g., *birdhouse, lighthouse, housefly; bookshelf, notebook, bookmark*).

Continued.

Kindergartners:	Grade 1 students:	Grade 2 students:
Vocabulary Acquisition and Use—cont'd		
		e. Use glossaries and beginning dictionaries, both print and digital, to determine or clarify the meaning of words and phrases.
5. With guidance and support from adults, explore word relationships and nuances in word meanings. a. Sort common objects into categories (e.g., shapes, foods) to gain a sense of the concepts the categories represent. b. Demonstrate understanding of frequently occurring verbs and adjectives by relating them to their opposites (antonyms). c. Identify real-life connections between words and their use (e.g., note places at school that are *colorful*). d. Distinguish shades of meaning among verbs describing the same general action (e.g., *walk, march, strut, prance*) by acting out the meanings.	5. With guidance and support from adults, demonstrate understanding of word relationships and nuances in word meanings. a. Sort words into categories (e.g., colors, clothing) to gain a sense of the concepts the categories represent. b. Define words by category and by one or more key attributes (e.g., a *duck* is a bird that swims; a *tiger* is a large cat with stripes). c. Identify real-life connections between words and their use (e.g., note places at home that are *cozy*). d. Distinguish shades of meaning among verbs differing in a manner (e.g., *look, peek, glance, stare, glare, scowl*) and adjectives differing in intensity (e.g., *large, gigantic*) by defining or choosing them or by acting out the meanings.	5. Demonstrate understanding of word relationships and nuances in word meanings. a. Identify real-life connections between words and their use (e.g., describe foods that are *spicy* or *juicy*). b. Distinguish shades of meaning among closely related verbs (e.g., *toss, throw, hurl*) and closely related adjectives (e.g., *thin, slender, skinny, scrawny*).
6. Use words and phrases acquired through conversations, reading and being read to, and responding to texts.	6. Use words and phrases acquired through conversations, reading and being read to, and responding to texts, including using frequently occurring conjunctions to signal simple relationships (e.g., *because*).	6. Use words and phrases acquired through conversations, reading and being read to, and responding to texts, including using adjectives and adverbs to describe (e.g., *When other kids are happy that makes me happy*).

Grade 3 students:	Grade 4 students:	Grade 5 students:
Conventions of Standard English		
1. Demonstrate command to the conventions of standard English grammar and usage when writing or speaking. a. Explain the function of nouns, pronouns, verbs, adjectives, and adverbs in general and their functions in particular sentences.	1. Demonstrate command to the conventions of standard English grammar and usage when writing or speaking. a. Use relative pronouns (*who, whose, whom, which, that*) and relative adverbs (*where, when, why*).	1. Demonstrate command to the conventions of standard English grammar and usage when writing or speaking. a. Explain the function of conjunctions, prepositions, and interjections in general and their function in particular sentences.

Grade 3 students:	Grade 4 students:	Grade 5 students:
Conventions of Standard English—cont'd		
b. Form and use regular and irregular plural nouns. c. Use abstract nouns (e.g., *childhood*). d. Form and use regular and irregular verbs. e. Form and use the simple (e.g., *I walked; I walk; I will walk*) verb tenses. f. Ensure subject-verb and pronoun-antecedent agreement. g. Form and use comparative and superlative adjectives and adverbs, and choose between them depending on what is to be modified. h. Use coordinating and subordinating conjunctions. i. Produce simple, compound, and complex sentences.	b. Form and use the progressive (e.g., *I was walking; I am walking; I will be walking*) verb tenses. c. Use modal auxiliaries (e.g., *can, may, must*) to convey various conditions. d. Order adjectives within sentences according to conventional patterns (e.g., *a small red bag* rather than *a red small bag*). e. Form and use prepositional phrases. f. Produce complete sentences, recognizing and correcting inappropriate fragments and run-ons. g. Correctly use frequently confused words (e.g., *to, too, two; there, their*).	b. Form and use the perfect (e.g., *I had walked; I have walked; I will have walked*) verb tenses. c. Use verb tense to convey various times, sequences, states, and conditions. d. Recognize and correct inappropriate shifts in verb tense. e. Use correlative conjunctions (e.g., *either/or, neither/nor*).

2. Demonstrate command of the conventions of standard English capitalization, punctuation, and spelling when writing.
  a. Capitalize appropriate words in titles.
  b. Use commas in addresses.
  c. Use commas and quotation marks in dialogue.
  d. Form and use possessives.
  e. Use conventional spelling for high-frequency and other studied words and for adding suffixes to base words (e.g., *sitting, smiled, cries, happiness*).
  f. Use spelling patterns and generalizations (e.g., word families, position-based spellings, syllable patterns, ending rules, meaningful word parts) in writing words.
  g. Consult reference materials, including beginning dictionaries, as needed to check and correct spellings.
	2. Demonstrate command of the conventions of standard English capitalization, punctuation, and spelling when writing.
	  a. Use correct capitalization.
	  b. Use commas and quotation marks to mark direct speech and quotations from a text.
	  c. Use a comma before a coordinating conjunction in a compound sentence.
	  d. Spell grade-appropriate words correctly, consulting references as needed.
		2. Demonstrate command of the conventions of standard English capitalization, punctuation, and spelling when writing.
		  a. Use punctuation to separate items in a series.
		  b. Use a comma to separate an introductory element from the rest of the sentence.
		  c. Use a comma to set off the words *yes* and *no* (e.g., *Yes, thank you*), to set off a tag question from the rest of the sentence (e.g., *It's true, isn't it?*), and to indicate direct address (e.g., *Is that you, Steve?*).
		  d. Use underlining, quotation marks, or italics to indicate titles of works.
		  e. Spell grade-appropriate words correctly, consulting references as needed.

Continued.

Grade 3 students:	Grade 4 students:	Grade 5 students:
Knowledge of Language		
3. Use knowledge of language and its conventions when writing, speaking, reading, or listening. a. Choose words and phrases for effect. b. Recognize and observe differences between the conventions of spoken and written standard English.	3. Use knowledge of language and its conventions when writing, speaking, reading, or listening. a. Choose words and phrases to convey ideas precisely. b. Choose punctuation for effect. c. Differentiate between contexts that call for formal English (e.g., presenting ideas) and situations where informal discourse is appropriate (e.g., small-group discussion).	3. Use knowledge of language and its conventions when writing, speaking, reading, or listening. a. Expand, combine, and reduce sentences for meaning, reader/listener interest, and style. b. Compare and contrast the varieties of English (e.g., dialects, registers) used in stories, dramas, or poems.

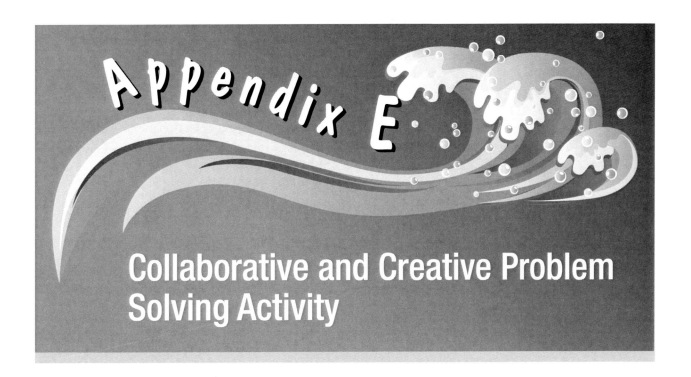

Collaborative and Creative Problem Solving Activity

Connecting reading and writing to the content areas is a natural thing to do. Important in the planning process is to include opportunities for students to be engaged collaboratively while solving problems in creative ways. One example of an interdisciplinary activity that incorporates writing, science, and social studies is Survival Island! Place students into groups of three or four. For each group, provide some newspapers, 3 ft. to 4 ft. long lengths of wire, masking tape, a 9-volt battery, and a small flashlight bulb. Hand out the scenario below to each group. Allow students to solve the problem of constructing a signaling device with only the materials given.

Theme:	**SURVIVAL ISLAND!**
Task:	**Building a rescue signal**
Scenario:	You and your fellow castaways have been shipwrecked off a tropical island in the South Seas of the Pacific Ocean. (You cannot assume that you washed ashore on Gilligan's Island and have the luxury of using the huts and other items created by Gilligan's fellow castaways!) After washing ashore, you and your group members gather your wits about you and begin to determine what you can do to get rescued. You are able to find some masking tape, newspapers that were bundled in plastic wrap that did not get delivered on your cruise, some wire, a battery, and a light bulb. Using these materials, you and your fellow castaways decide that the best thing to do is to try to construct a signaling device that can be seen from the beach by passing ships off shore.

With your group, brainstorm what you can create and how to create it. Will different members have different jobs? After making plans, begin to build your signal! Good luck!

Remember, you are stranded on an island with no paper and pencils at this time! As you work together, make mental notes of various things, such as:

- Does anyone assume a leadership role?
- How are your materials working for you?
- How are you adapting the task based on the materials you have?
- What steps is your group going through to complete the task?

Post Scenario Journaling: Respond to the following—What was the most difficult part of the process for you? What was the easiest part? How did you and your group work together to construct the signaling device? Did anyone take over as the leader of the group? If so, how did that person do as a leader? Did your signaling device work? Why or why not?

Activity Debriefing (For university students engaged in the activity):

Consider the following:
- How can this approach be used in an elementary classroom to integrate social studies, science, language arts, and other subject areas?
- How did civics come into play?
- How did economics come into play?
- Could you use this scenario with elementary students? If so, what grade(s)?
- How might you expand on the theme of survival and use other texts to incorporate survival in a variety of contexts?

Reading/Writing Interview—
Grades 3–6

Name _____ Age _____ Grade in School _____

1. In general, how do you feel about reading? How do you feel about writing?

2. What kinds of things do you like to read? What kinds of things do you like to write about?

3. What are your favorite types/genres of books to read? Check the ones you like best.
   ☐ animal stories   ☐ mystery books   ☐ historical fiction   ☐ realistic fiction
   ☐ legends/myths   ☐ folktales   ☐ informational books   ☐ fantasy
   ☐ science fiction ☐ poetry   ☐ biography/autobiography   ☐ how-to books

4. How many books would you say are in your house? What other kinds of things are in your home that you can read?

5. How often do you read at home? How often do you write at home?

6. Have you ever read the same book more than once? If so, can you name it (them)?

7. How do you feel about spending free time reading (writing)?

8. Do you read to anyone in your home? If so, who? Why do you read to this person?

9. Do you read with your mother or father at home? Do you like to read with him/her? Why or why not?

10. What do you think parents should do to help their children with reading (with writing)?

11. What do you do when you come to a word or sentence that you do not understand when you are reading?

12. What do you do when you are writing and you want to use a word you are not sure how to spell?

13. Do you think it is important to become a good reader (writer)? Why or why not?

14. What do you want to be when you grow up? Why? Do you think reading and writing will be important in your future career?

(Adapted from Snyder, A.F. (2003). *An examination of reading interactions between mothers and their daughters in grades four through six.* Unpublished doctoral dissertation, University of Pittsburgh, Pittsburgh, PA.)